SEO 2023
LEARN SEARCH ENGINE OPTIMIZATION
WITH SMART INTERNET MARKETING STRATEGIES

Expanded & Updated

Adam Clarke

Simple Effectiveness Publishing, Publisher.
Cover Design: Simple Effectiveness Publishing.
Production and Composition: Simple Effectiveness Publishing.

Adam Clarke completed a Digital Marketing certificate from Google's Digital Garage accredited by the Interactive Advertising Bureau Europe and The Open University and is a member of the Digital Analytics Association.

SEO 2023: Learn search engine optimization with smart internet marketing strategies.
Adam Clarke
Kindle ASIN B00NH0XZR0

TABLE OF CONTENTS.

3. On-page SEO. How to let Google know what your page is about.

- How to structure your site for easy and automatic SEO.
- How to make Google pick up the keywords you want.
- How to get more people clicking on your rankings in Google.
- Load speed—Google magic dust.
- The usual suspects—sitemaps.xml and robots.txt.
- Duplicate content—canonical tags and other fun.
- Usability—the new SEO explained.
- Mobile support—important SEO explained in simple language.
- Google's Search Quality Guidelines—and how to use them to your advantage.
- Readability—SEO for the future.
- How to accelerate traffic and rankings with content marketing.
- HTTPS & SSL upgrade checklist.
- User Behavior Optimization—how to use Google's machine learning technology to your advantage.
- Google's Core Web Vitals.

4. Link building. How to rank extremely high on Google.

- Why is link-building so important?
- The dirty little secret no one wants to tell you about link building.
- How to acquire links and what to avoid in link building.
- Anchor text. What's all the fuss?
- Simple to advanced link-building strategies.
- Link outreach—scaling up high-quality link-building campaigns.
- How to get links from major news outlets for free.
- Additional link-building opportunities.

Bonus chapter 2: The quick and dirty guide to pay-per-click advertising with Google Ads.
- Why bother with pay-per-click advertising?
- Which is the best PPC provider to start with?
- Ensuring success with research and a plan.
- How to choose the right kind of keywords.
- Structuring your campaign with ad groups.
- How to crush the competition with killer text ads.
- How much to pay for keywords.
- Google Ads settings for getting started.
- Optimization tips for tweaking your campaign for better profit.
- Using Accelerated Mobile Pages in Google Ads campaigns to accelerate your sales.
- Further Google Ads resources.

Bonus: 50-point SEO Checklist PDF instructions.

Final thoughts & tips.

FREE SEO CHECKLIST PDF AND FREE VIDEO TUTORIALS ARE AVAILABLE AT THE END OF THIS BOOK.

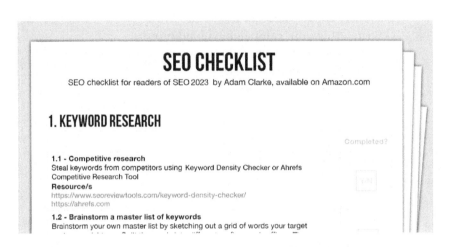

The free 50-point SEO 2023 - SEO Checklist PDF, covers exact steps to improve your website's ranking in Google, and free video tutorials, are available for readers at the end of this book. Instructions on accessing the SEO checklist PDF and video tutorials are at the end of the book.

INTRODUCTION TO THE UPDATED EDITION.

So, you've picked up SEO 2023 and decided to learn search engine optimization. Congratulations! SEO marketing has changed my life and it will change yours too.

Over 20 years ago, I achieved my first number-one ranking in Google for my family's home business. The phone started ringing with new customers every day and I was hooked.

Since then, I have used search engine optimization to grow hotel chains, large international fashion brands, and small family-owned businesses. One thing never ceases to amaze me—the power of SEO for growing any business. I have grown small businesses into giant companies in just one or two years, simply by working the site up to the top position in Google.

Unfortunately, learning SEO and Internet marketing is difficult for many business owners, Internet marketers, and tech heads.

I have a theory on why this is so...

Sifting through the information flooding the Internet about SEO is overwhelming. In many cases, advice online is outdated or misleading. And the constant updates by Google make it hard for SEO beginners and gurus alike to keep up with what works.

SEO can be simple and used by anyone to rank at the top of Google, grow their business, and make money online. It's a matter of having up-to-date information on how Google works, using effective techniques, and taking action.

This book has been expanded and updated to cover how SEO works now and likely in the future. All of the resources and tools have been updated and made relevant for 2023. It includes broader coverage of the basics and is filled with more techniques for advanced users. And due to requests by readers, it has been loaded with more tools and resources to save time and get bigger results.

If you are a beginner, there is a small amount of technical information included in this book. If you want to learn search engine optimization this can't be avoided. We've made these areas as simple as possible, while providing additional resources, including an SEO checklist, that will speed up your journey to SEO mastery.

If you are an advanced SEO optimization professional, this SEO book covers Google's latest updates, new SEO marketing best practices to refresh your memory, solutions for common technical problems, and new tools and resources to sharpen your skillset — all written in an easy-to-read format, so refreshing your knowledge doesn't feel like a chore.

Whether you're a complete SEO beginner or a seasoned Internet marketing veteran, SEO 2023 covers these areas and makes it as simple as possible to achieve rankings, traffic, and sales.

Enjoy.

1. INTRODUCTION TO HOW GOOGLE WORKS.

You can feel like a dog chasing its tail trying to figure out how Google works.

There are thousands of bloggers and journalists spreading volumes of information that simply isn't true. If you followed all the advice about SEO written on blogs, it's unlikely you would receive top listings in Google, and there's a risk you could damage your site performance and make it difficult to rank at all.

Let me tell you a secret about bloggers...

Articles about the latest SEO updates, techniques, or tips are often written by interns, assistants, and ghostwriters. Their job is to write articles. The majority of blog posts about SEO are rarely written by experts or professionals with the day-to-day responsibility of growing site traffic and achieving top rankings in search engines.

Can you learn from someone who doesn't know how to do it themselves?

You can't. This is why you have to take the advice spread by blog posts with a grain of salt.

Don't get me wrong. I love bloggers. There are bloggers out there who practice and blog about SEO and do it well. But it has become increasingly difficult to sort the wheat from the chaff.

Fear not. This chapter will disperse common misconceptions about SEO, show you how to avoid falling into Google's bad books and reveal how to stay up to date with how Google ranks sites.

But first, to understand how Google works today, we must understand a little bit about Google's history.

OLD-SCHOOL METHODS NO LONGER WORK.

In the early days of Google—around 25 years ago—Google started a smarter search engine and a better experience for navigating the World Wide Web. Google delivered on this promise by delivering relevant search results.

Internet users discovered they could simply type what they were looking for into Google—and BINGO—users would find what they needed in the top results, instead of having to dig through hundreds of pages. Google's user base grew fast.

It didn't take long for smart and entrepreneurially minded webmasters to catch on to sneaky little hacks for ranking high in Google.

Webmasters discovered by cramming many keywords into the page, they could get their site to rank high for almost any word or phrase. It quickly spiraled into a competition of who could jam the most keywords into the page. The page with the most repeated keywords won and rose swiftly to the top of the search results.

Naturally, more and more spammers caught on and Google's promise as the "most relevant search engine" was challenged. Webmasters and spammers became more sophisticated and found tricky ways of repeating hundreds of keywords on the page and completely hiding them from human eyes.

All of a sudden, the unsuspecting Internet user looking for "holidays in Florida", would find themselves arriving at a website about Viagra, Viagra, Viagra!

How could Google keep its status as the most relevant search engine, if people kept on spamming the results with gazillions of spammy pages, burying relevant results to the bottom?

Enter the first Google update. Google released a widespread update in November 2003, codenamed "Florida", effectively stopping spammers in their tracks. This update leveled the playing field by rendering keyword stuffing useless and restored balance to the force.

And so began the long history of Google updates — making it hard for spammers to game the system, and making ranking in Google a little more complicated.

GOOGLE UPDATES AND HOW TO SURVIVE THEM.

Fast forward 25 years and ranking in Google became extremely competitive and complex.

Simply put, everybody wants to be in Google. Google is fighting to keep its search engine relevant and must constantly evolve to continue delivering relevant results to users.

This hasn't been without its challenges. Just like keyword stuffing, webmasters eventually clued onto another way of gaming the system by having the most "anchor text" pointing to the page.

If you're not familiar with this term, anchor text is the text contained in external links pointing to a page.

This created another loophole exploited by spammers. And in some cases, well-meaning marketers and business owners use this tactic to rank high in Google's search results.

Along came a new Google update in 2012, this time called "Penguin". Google's Penguin update punished sites with suspicious amounts of links with the same anchor text pointing to a page, by completely delisting sites from the search results. Many businesses that relied on search engine traffic lost all of their sales, literally overnight, because Google believed sites with hundreds of links containing one phrase didn't acquire those links naturally. Google believed this was a solid indicator the site owner could be gaming the system.

If you find these changes alarming, don't. How to recover from these changes, or to prevent being penalized by new updates, is covered in later chapters. In the short history of Google's major updates, we can discover two powerful lessons for achieving top rankings in Google.

1. If you want to stay at the top of Google, never rely on one tactic.

2. Always ensure your search engine strategies rely on SEO best practices.

AUTHORITY, TRUST, RELEVANCE & USER EXPERIENCE. FOUR NEW POWERFUL SEO STRATEGIES EXPLAINED.

Google considerably evolved from its humble origins in 1998.

Eric Schmidt, the former CEO of Google, once reported Google considers over 200 factors to determine which sites rank higher in the results.

Today, Google uses well over 200 factors. Google assesses how users are behaving on your site, how many links are pointing to your site, how trustworthy these linking sites are, how many social mentions your brand has, how relevant your page is, how old your site is, how fast your site loads… the list goes on.

Does this mean it's impossible or difficult to get top rankings in Google?

No. In fact, you have the advantage.

Google's algorithm is complex, but you don't have to be a rocket scientist to understand how it works. It can be ridiculously simple if you remember just four principles. With these four principles, you can determine why one site ranks higher than another or discover what you have to do to push your site higher than a competitor.

Some of these principles have been around for donkey's years, and others just added in the past year or so, but these four principles summarize what Google is focusing on in the algorithm now, and are the most powerful strategies SEO professionals currently use to rank high in search engines.

The four areas of focus are Trust, Authority, Relevance, and User Experience.

1. Trust.

Trust is at the very core of Google's major changes and updates over the past couple of years. Google wants to keep poor-quality, untrustworthy sites out of the search results, and keep high-quality, legit sites at the top. If your site has well-researched, high-quality content and backlinks from reputable sources, your site is more likely to be a trustworthy source. If your site has a real business address, contact information, and real people listed on an about page, your page is more likely to be trustworthy, and likely to rank higher in the search results.

2. Authority

Previously the most popular SEO strategy, authority is still powerful, but now best used in tandem with the other two principles. Authority is your site's overall strength in your market. Authority is almost a numbers game, for example: if your site has one thousand social media followers and backlinks, and your competitors only have fifty social media followers and backlinks, you're probably going to rank higher.

3. Relevance.

Google looks at the contextual relevance of a site and rewards relevant sites with higher rankings. This levels the playing field a bit and explains why a niche site or local business can often rank higher than a Wikipedia article. You can use this to your advantage by bulking out the content of your site with relevant content and using the on-page SEO techniques described in later chapters, to give Google a nudge to see your site is relevant. You can rank higher with fewer links by building links from relevant sites. Increasing relevance like this is a powerful strategy and can lead to high rankings in competitive areas.

4. User Experience.

Are users sticking to your content like glue? Or are they visiting and leaving your site faster than Usain Bolt?... How users behave on your site tells Google if they are having a positive experience. Simply, Google wants sites at the top of the results to deliver a positive user experience.

User behavior and user experience are quite new but are now among the strongest factors in Google's algorithm.

You can take advantage of this by improving your website's user experience — techniques covered later in this book.

HOW GOOGLE RANKS SITES RIGHT NOW—GOOGLE'S NEWEST TOP 10 RANKING FACTORS REVEALED.

You may have wondered if you can find out the exact factors in Google's algorithm.

Fortunately, there are a handful of industry leaders who have figured it out and regularly publish their findings on the Internet. With these publications, you can get a working knowledge of the factors Google uses to rank sites. These surveys are typically updated every couple of years, but the biggest factors don't often change, so you can use them to your advantage by knowing which areas to focus on.

Here's a short list of the current strongest factors in the top 10 search results, according to recent industry studies:

- Consistent publication of engaging content
- Keywords in meta title tags
- Backlinks
- Niche expertise
- User engagement
- Trustworthiness
- Mobile-friendly / mobile-first website
- Internal links
- Page speed
- Site security / SSL certificate

If your competitors have more of the above features than yours, they will likely rank higher than you. If you have more of the above features than competitors, you will likely rank higher.

Combine this knowledge with an understanding of the Google updates covered in later chapters, and you will know what it takes to achieve top rankings.

The above ranking factors are from the following industry survey. If you want a deeper look into recent studies, you can browse the full reports by searching for "Google Ranking Factors" in Google. I also cover the newest updates to Google's algorithm in the Google Algorithm updates chapter later in this book.

The 2023 Google Algorithm Ranking Factors - First Page Sage
https://firstpagesage.com/seo-blog/the-google-algorithm-ranking-factors/

GOOGLE'S MOBILE-FIRST INDEX.

Historically, Google primarily used the desktop version of a page's content when calculating the search results. Since the majority of users now access Google via a mobile device, Google primarily relies on the mobile version of a page's content to calculate the results.

Want simple language? Google is now using the mobile version of websites as the first touchpoint in calculating the search results, for both desktop and mobile devices... Hold up a minute... Did I just say that the mobile version of your site is the FIRST touchpoint for calculating BOTH results... Damn straight!

It makes sense when you think about it. The vast majority of the Internet's users are mobile users. To ensure smartphone addicts are delivered with better results on the move, it makes sense for Google to make mobile the highest priority in the algorithm, with desktops quickly becoming a minority of Internet users.

If you haven't jumped on the mobile bandwagon by now — with mobile traffic making up around 70%-80% of traffic for most sites — you're missing out on traffic right this very second and you may eventually completely fall off the mobile results.

Fortunately, there's an elegant solution discussed in the mobile SEO section in the on-page SEO chapter, but I'll let Google spokesperson Gary Illyes take the reins, with a direct quote from a discussion about this technology...

"If you have a responsive site, then you're pretty much good to go. Why? Because the content on your desktop site will be pretty much the same as on your responsive site. The structured data on your desktop site will be the same."

In other words, if your site is responsive and supports mobile users, you can lie back and enjoy a Piña Colada, knowing your desktop-only competitors will eventually fall to the wayside, while you bask in the glory of a mobile-first paradise for users.

GOOGLE'S USE OF MACHINE LEARNING TECHNOLOGY TO POWER THE SEARCH RESULTS.

When Google announced its machine-learning technology titled RankBrain, RankBrain had been influencing search results secretly for several months. Does this mean sinister super-intelligent robots created by the genius minds at Google are slowly taking over our search results?... Well, not really.

Over 15% of Google's daily searches have never been searched before. On these never-before-seen types of searches, Google doesn't have any historic data to ensure it is delivering the right answer. Understandably, Google needs a strong capability to understand the actual meaning behind a user's query as they type it into the search box, even if it has never been searched.

Enter RankBrain, RankBrain forms connections between words to get a better understanding of what a searcher wants, when the searcher only gives Google a small amount of information. It then delivers a relevant answer, even when the best answers don't use the exact words the user searched for.

In the above example, simply by searching "fastest runner" the first search result lists Usain Bolt at the top of the search results. That's some solid guesswork from Google! We can see Google's strong capability at inferring the actual meaning behind our search, even though I only hinted at the person I am searching about. This is Google's RankBrain technology at work, forming connections behind the scenes. As popular trends come and go, this matching technology is automatically applied in new searches and organically changes to adapt to the times.

Ever since Google's release of RankBrain, Google has been gradually working new A.I. and machine learning technologies into the search results. The new technologies help Google to understand more complicated searches, deliver more relevant results to users' questions, and strengthen Google's status as the world's most advanced search engine.

The overall impact on business and website owners has been positive, allowing websites to show up at the top of the search results for more searches.

GOOGLE UNDERSTANDS HOW HUMANS SPEAK.

Let's face it, we're getting lazy about how we use the Internet. Getting the laptop out feels like a drag and we're shouting shorthand voice searches into our phones like, "movie 1990s people experiment dying kiefer sutherland", expecting Google to do the heavy lifting...

And it does! Displaying the Wikipedia entry for the 1990's film "Flatliners", a cult classic about medical students experimenting with near-death-experiences. On the Flatliners Wikipedia page, the word "experiment" appears only once, but Kiefer Sutherland appeared in over 29 movies in the 1990s, in which lots of characters died. Notice how I accidentally typed in 1980s and Google figured it out, anyway? Solid work by Google.

To combat increasing ambiguity in searches, with 15 percent of searches being entirely brand new—and just getting a better grasp on human language—Google developed the biggest leap forward in search technology since RankBrain called... BERT.

Or for short, Bidirectional Encoder Representations from Transformers... A machine-learning technology to better understand human language.

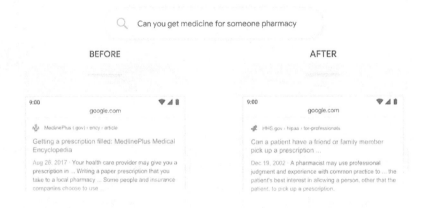

Before BERT, Google would previously struggle with searches like "can you get medicine for someone pharmacy", delivering a non-specific result about getting prescriptions filled.

After BERT, Google understands the searcher's intent better, now delivering a result about whether a patient can send a friend or family member to get their prescription filled.

Some takeaways about this groundbreaking technology by Google:

- BERT is entirely focused on better understanding the way humans communicate (a type of machine learning called Natural Language Processing).
- Searches affected include queries with Homonyms and Polysemes (e.g. the verb "run" is a Polyseme, with 606 different-but-similar meanings according to the Oxford Dictionary).
- Other searches affected include conversational or shorthand queries — such as "parking on a hill with no curb." The last part of this search transforms the intent of the search. This is where the "Bidirectional" aspect of BERT's algorithm comes into play.
- Top-performing sites didn't report any major losses or gains in traffic and rankings after the update.
- Pages targeting long-tail searches will most likely benefit from this update.

SEO professionals industry-wide analyzed the technology upside-down and back-to-front to find an edge... And the consensus is not much to do, besides making sure your page shows high-quality content, including related keywords, LSI keywords, and natural language on your pages... And perhaps targeting more long-tail keywords.

HOW TO STAY AHEAD OF GOOGLE'S UPDATES.

Now and then, Google releases a significant update to its algorithm, which can have a massive impact on businesses from any industry. To hone your SEO chops and make sure your site doesn't fall into Google's bad books, it's important to stay informed of Google's updates as they are released.

Fortunately, almost every time a major update is released, those updates are reported on by the entire SEO community and sometimes publicly discussed and confirmed by Google staff.

A long-extended history of Google's updates would fill this entire book. But with the resources below, you can stay abreast of new Google updates as they are rolled out. This is essential knowledge for anyone practicing SEO, at a beginner or advanced level.

Keep your ear to the ground with these sources and you'll often be forewarned of future updates.

Search Engine Round Table
https://www.seroundtable.com/

Search Engine Round Table is a blog that covers the daily happenings in the world of SEO. The author, Barry Schwartz, provides breakdowns and summaries of Google's updates and is often one of the first places to break news on major changes in the SEO industry.

List of Google Search Ranking Updates - Google Search Central
https://developers.google.com/search/updates/ranking

Wouldn't it be great if there was an official page where Google announces its major updates to Google search? Well, there is. Google maintains an official list of all the major updates (that Google wants us to know about). It's a good resource to visit because whenever Google releases a massive update, you can read the official documentation and guidelines about what to do instead of playing guessing games.

The Keyword - Google
https://blog.google/

Google's public blog, The Keyword, publishes Google's major news and announcements. Often big changes are reported here by Google before they are rolled out, which makes it an important resource for staying up to date.

2. KEYWORD RESEARCH. THE MOST IMPORTANT STEP OF SEO.

WHY IS KEYWORD RESEARCH SO IMPORTANT?

Keyword research is the most important step of every SEO project for two reasons:

1. To discover keywords with traffic. Otherwise, you could waste lots of time and effort trying to rank for keywords that don't generate any traffic.

2. To find keywords that are easy to rank high in the search results. If you don't investigate keyword competitiveness, you can waste lots of time and effort on a keyword only to find it is far too difficult to rank on the first page.

These two goals are the ultimate decider of how successful an SEO project is.

This chapter will cover how to find the best keywords and how to avoid spending time on the wrong keywords. First, we must define what a keyword is.

WHAT EXACTLY IS A KEYWORD?

If you are an SEO newbie, you may be wondering—what is a keyword?

A keyword is any phrase you would like your site to rank for in Google's search results. A keyword can be a single word, or a keyword can also be a combination of words. If you are trying to target a single word, look out! You will have your work cut out for you. Single-word keywords are extremely competitive and difficult to rank highly for in the search results.

Here are some different kinds of keywords:

Head-term keywords: keywords with one to two words, i.e. classic movies.

Long-tail keywords: keywords with three or more phrases, i.e. classic Akira Kurosawa movies.

Navigational keywords: keywords used to locate a brand or website. Examples would be Facebook, YouTube, or Gmail.

Informational keywords: keywords used to find information about a particular topic. This includes keywords beginning with "how to..." or "what are the best..."

Transactional keywords: keywords entered into Google by customers wanting to complete a commercial activity, i.e. buy jackets online.

In most cases, targeting head-term or navigational keywords for other brands is competitive and not worth the time or effort. Despite their high traffic numbers, they will generally not lead to any sales. On the other hand, long-tail, informational, and transactional keywords are good keywords for most SEO projects. They will lead to more customers.

HOW TO GENERATE A MASSIVE LIST OF KEYWORDS.

There are many ways to skin a cat. The same is true for finding the right keywords.

Before you can find keywords with loads of traffic in Google, you must first develop a list of potential keywords relevant to your business.

Relevance is vital.

If you spend your time trying to cast too wide a net, you can end up targeting keywords irrelevant to your audience.

For example, if you are an online football jacket retailer in the United States, examples of relevant keywords might be:

Buy football jackets
Buy football jackets online
Online football jackets store USA

Irrelevant keywords might be:

Football jacket photos
How to make your own football jacket
Football jacket manufacturers
How to design a football jacket

You can see how the first pool of keywords is more relevant to the target audience of football jacket retailers, and the second pool of keywords is related but unlikely to lead to customers.

Keeping relevance in mind, you must develop a list of potential keyword combinations to use as a resource, so you can then go and uncover the best keywords with a decent amount of traffic each month in Google.

Here are some powerful strategies you can use to generate this list.

1. Steal keywords from competitors.

If you're feeling sneaky, you can let your competitors do the heavy lifting for you and snatch up keywords from their sites.

There are many tools out there created for this purpose. A simple, free tool is the Keyword Density Checker. If you enter a page into this tool, within seconds, it will scrape a list of the keywords your competitor has optimized into their page. You can then use this to bulk out your keyword list.

Keyword Density Checker – SEO Review Tools
https://www.seoreviewtools.com/keyword-density-checker/

While the Keyword Density Checker is a lightweight tool for revealing keywords your competitors have optimized into the page, a more robust tool is Ahrefs' Organic Keywords report. This tool estimates the keywords that are sending the largest amount of traffic to competitors' websites. The estimates are reasonably accurate and are a valuable resource for bulking keyword lists.

While Ahrefs reports are powerful, they come at a cost. Monthly plans start at $99 per month.

Ahrefs
https://ahrefs.com

2. Use AI chatbot tools like ChatGPT and Google's Bard to generate keyword ideas.

When it comes to generating keyword ideas, AI chatbot tools like ChatGPT and Google's Bard save a lot of time and effort.

These tools can churn out relevant and unique keyword ideas faster than you can say "Hail Mary," making your SEO game plan much easier to execute.

Let's put ChatGPT to the test with NFL merchandise as our focus.

When we input "Give me a list of 30 core keywords for an NFL merchandise store, that sells NFL Jerseys, NFL jackets, and so on," ChatGPT flexes its AI muscles and returns this list of NFL-related keywords...

- NFL merchandise.
- Football gear.
- NFL jerseys.
- Team apparel.
- NFL jackets.
- Sports memorabilia.
- Fan clothing.
- Official team wear.
- NFL hats.
- NFL accessories.
- NFL shop.
- Football fanwear.
- Game day gear.
- Team spirit.
- NFL hoodies.
- NFL collectibles.
- NFL gifts.
- NFL t-shirts.
- Football accessories.
- Custom NFL jerseys.
- NFL sweatshirts.

- NFL caps.
- Player jerseys.
- NFL tailgating gear.
- NFL scarves.
- NFL bags.
- Football equipment.
- NFL team flags.
- NFL home decor.
- Licensed NFL products.

While the keyword suggestions are nothing short of excellent, the one thing you have to keep in mind with generative AI chatbots like ChatGPT is that you can't trust the accuracy of the data.

By all means, get keyword ideas, just don't trust any traffic or SEO difficulty estimates that come out of these tools — we'll cover how to get those in a minute anyways.

3. Brainstorm a master list of keywords.

Assuming competitors have been thorough with their research isn't always the best strategy. By brainstorming combinations of keywords, you can generate a giant list of potential keywords.

To do this, sketch out a grid of words your target customer might use. Split the words into different prefixes and suffixes. Next up, combine them into one giant list using the free Mergewords tool. With this strategy, you can quickly and easily build up a massive list of relevant keywords.

Mergewords
https://www.toptal.com/marketing/mergewords

Prefix
- buy
- where do I buy

Middle word
- NFL jerseys
- NFL uniforms
- NFL jackets

Suffixes
- online

Combined keywords
- NFL jerseys
- NFL jerseys online
- NFL uniforms
- NFL uniforms online
- NFL jackets
- NFL jackets online
- buy NFL jerseys
- buy NFL jerseys online
- buy NFL uniforms
- buy NFL uniforms online
- buy NFL jackets
- buy NFL jackets online
- where do I buy NFL jerseys
- where do I buy NFL jerseys online
- where do I buy NFL uniforms
- where do I buy NFL uniforms online
- where do I buy NFL jackets

- where do I buy NFL jackets online
- NFL jerseys
- NFL jerseys online
- NFL uniforms
- NFL uniforms online
- NFL jackets
- NFL jackets online

4. Going undercover and researching your niche.

With 4.54 billion active Internet users—even if you're selling leopard print dog watches—there's a community of people floating around on the web interested in what you're selling... You've just got to go and find them.

Open up a few tabs and browse through online communities like Reddit, Quora, Facebook Groups, Slack communities, and Twitter hashtags, going through popular threads. Keep a close eye on popular and trending topics, and questions with a tendency to resurface. You'll find burning questions needing to be answered, generating the best kind of keyword ideas—ideas directly from customers' keyboards. You can discover additional niche-specific forums with the following search queries:

"keyword" forums
"keyword" discussion board
"keyword" community

5. Use tools that reveal hidden trends on the web.

Researching Internet trends and getting insights behind Google's search box isn't a new idea, and fortunately, clever people have built powerful tools for making this job easy. Add these tools to your keyword research arsenal. Not only will you save precious time researching, but you'll also receive a ton of relevant suggestions you wouldn't discover otherwise.

Ubersuggest.
https://neilpatel.com/ubersuggest/
No SEO guide would be complete without mentioning Ubersuggest. This handy tool reveals autocomplete suggestions behind Google's search box. It provides region-specific data for countries and languages all around the globe, and the best part—it's free.

Answer The Public
https://answerthepublic.com/
Answer The Public crawls the Internet and generates automatic lists of customers burning questions related to your keyword. Answer The Public starts with phrases starting with common question-type words, such as "how", "when", "can", and so on, followed by your keyword. It provides long lists of phrases containing prepositions, such as "can", "is", "with", and "without", preceded by your keyword. And topping things off, it lists common questions users type in Google, from a-to-z, after your keyword (postpositions, if you want to talk fancy). In other words, it's a giant database of questions customers are asking about your topic.

Buzzsumo

https://buzzsumo.com/

Sometimes, ideas become popular on the Internet before being typed into Google's search box. You can get ahead of these trends with content discovery tools like Buzzsumo. Buzzsumo lists content going viral over the Internet right now. You can keep your finger on the pulse of what's hot across the web even when other tools haven't picked it up yet.

Use the above tools and you'll have more than enough keywords, and you'll be ready to start finding which keywords have solid amounts of traffic to send to your site.

HOW TO FIND KEYWORDS THAT WILL SEND TRAFFIC TO YOUR SITE.

Now you have a list of keywords, you need to understand how much traffic these keywords receive in Google. Without search traffic data, you could end up targeting keywords with zero searches. Armed with the right knowledge, you can target keywords with hundreds or thousands of potential visitors every month.

Unfortunately, in recent years Google restricted access to the data behind Google's search box, leaving us with two options for finding keyword traffic data.

Firstly, if you have a Google Ads campaign running with Google and are already spending a modest amount, then you're in the clear, you can access this info for free in their Keyword Planner tool. If this isn't you, the other option is to use a paid keyword research tool for a small monthly fee, such as keywordtool.io. As a result of Google making search data unavailable to free users, free keyword tools disappeared from the market, making paid research tools the only viable option for finding traffic data for keywords these days.

If you're on a tight budget, then you can sign up for a paid plan with one of the many paid keyword research tools on the market and then ask for a refund after doing your research. It's not nice, but it's an option—either way, you need the traffic data behind your keywords otherwise you are running blind.

1. Estimating keyword traffic data with Google's Keyword Planner.

Google Ads Keyword Planner
https://ads.google.com/home/tools/keyword-planner/

As mentioned, to access all the juicy traffic data provided by the Google Ads Keyword Planner tool, you need an active Google Ads campaign running and must be spending a modest amount of money regularly.

If this is you, sign in, click on Tools in the top menu, click on "Keyword Planner" then click on "Get search volume data and forecasts", and copy and paste your keywords into the box. Select your country, and then click the blue "Get started" button. When finished, you will have the exact amount of times each keyword was searched for in Google.

Mmm. Fresh data. This is just the kind of data we need.

Now we know which keywords receive more searches than others, and more importantly, we know which keywords receive no searches at all.

Keyword	Clicks	↓ Impressions	Cost	CTR
[football jerseys]	1,761.27	20,014.10	A$3,036.48	8.8%
[football jackets]	85.57	1,001.40	A$52.36	8.5%
[football jerseys online]	21.28	146.43	A$25.34	14.5%
[where to buy football jerseys]	0.35	5.14	A$1.22	6.9%

2. Estimating keyword traffic data with a paid tool like KWFinder or Ahrefs.

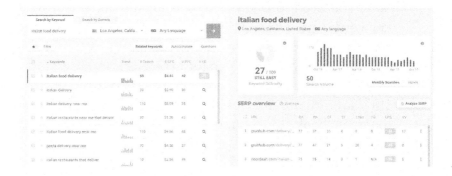

KWFinder
https://kwfinder.com/

If you want a research tool with a stronger SEO focus, then you can use a paid tool such as KWFinder or Ahrefs. You're not limited to these tools, many alternatives are floating around that you can find with a couple of Google searches.

Using KWFinder as an example, after creating an account, simply log in, select the local area you are targeting (i.e. Los Angeles, California, if that is your focus), enter your keyword ideas, and download the juicy data. Now you can ensure you spend time focusing on keywords with traffic potential, as opposed to chasing after keywords with no traffic and no opportunity for growing your business.

HOW TO FIND KEYWORDS FOR EASY RANKINGS.

Now you need to find out how competitive your desired keywords are. Armed with an understanding of the competitiveness of your keywords, you can discover keywords you can rank high for in Google.

Let's say you are a second-hand bookseller and you want to target "book store online." It's unlikely you are going to beat Amazon and Barnes and Noble.

But, maybe there's a gem hiding in your keyword list few people are targeting. Something like "antique book stores online."

You have the advantage if your competitors haven't thought of targeting your keyword. You simply have to do better SEO than they are doing and you have a really good chance of beating their rankings. Part of this includes having a large keyword list for your research.

Next, you need to wash this list and separate the ridiculously competitive keywords from the easy keywords no one is aggressively targeting.

There are many schools of thought on how to find the competitiveness of your keywords. The most popular practices are listed below, with my thoughts on each.

1. Manually going through the list, looking at the rankings, and checking if low-quality pages are appearing in the top results.

This is good for a glance to see how competitive a market is. However, unreliable and you need real data to rely on.

2. Look at how many search engine results are coming up in Google for your keyword.

The amount of results is listed just below the search box after you type in your keyword. This tactic is common in outdated courses teaching SEO and is completely unreliable.

The reason? There may be a very low number of competing pages for a particular keyword, but the sites ranked at the top of the results could be unbeatable.

3. Using the competition score from the Google Ads Keyword Planner tool.

Don't be tempted. This is a common beginner's mistake, and sometimes recommended as an easy way to judge SEO competitiveness for keywords on some blogs, and it just simply doesn't work!

The competition score included in the Google Ads Keyword Research tool is intended for Google Ads advertising campaigns only. It is an indication of how many advertisers are competing for a particular keyword through paid advertising. Completely irrelevant to SEO.

4. Using an SEO competitive analysis tool, such as KWFinder's SEO Difficulty report or Ahref's SEO Difficulty Score.

Now we're talking. To get a realistic idea of your chances of ranking high for a particular keyword, you need to understand the strength of the pages currently ranking in the top 10 search results for that keyword.

A great tool for this is KWFinder's SEO Difficulty report. With KWFinder's SEO Difficulty report, enter your keyword into their tool, click "check difficulty", and it will show vital stats for pages appearing in the top 10.

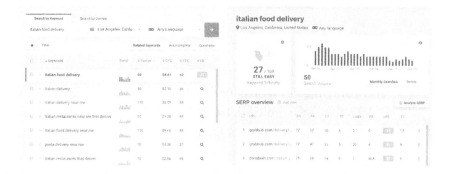

Of these stats, the most important are Domain Authority, Page Authority, Links, and Facebook Shares... If you don't have high Domain Authority or Page Authority—don't freak out. If your site is more relevant to the topic, you can often nudge your way up the results by creating great content, focusing on building backlinks to your page, and improving your social media activity.

Alternatively, Ahrefs has a great keyword difficulty score with its keyword tool. Enter your keywords into the Ahrefs keyword tool, and you can get a general idea of how difficult it will be to rank high for those keywords, by looking at the SEO difficulty score for each keyword.

You can also enter your website into Ahref's Site Explorer tool, enter your competitor's sites into Ahref's Site Explorer, and set targets for beating the competition. This a great strategy for more difficult keywords.

Ahrefs
https://ahrefs.com/

You can find keywords competitors are using, how much traffic they are getting from those keywords, and even where they get their links from!

Many keyword tools and site analysis tools can be found with a couple of Google searches. Every SEO professional ultimately has a different favorite tool they prefer, but in general, you'll find that Ahrefs is used for intermediate to advanced SEO professionals, and Moz's Keyword Explorer and KW Finder are used by beginners.

When finished reading this book, you can work through the keyword research points in the free SEO checklist included at the end of the book, with the process outlined in a step-by-step approach.

3. ON-PAGE SEO. HOW TO LET GOOGLE KNOW WHAT YOUR PAGE IS ABOUT.

On-page SEO is the process of ensuring your site is readable to search engines. Learning correct on-page SEO is important in ensuring Google picks up the keywords you want, and an opportunity to achieve easy wins and improve your site's overall performance.

On-page SEO has the following goals or actions:

1. Ensuring your site content is visible to search engines.
2. Ensuring your site is not blocking search engines.
3. Ensuring search engines pick up the keywords you want.
4. Ensuring site visitors are having a positive user experience.

You can do most on-page SEO yourself if you have experience working on websites.

If you are not technically inclined, please note there are technical sections in this chapter. You should read these so you understand what has to be done to achieve rankings in Google. You can easily hire a web designer or web developer to implement the techniques in this chapter after you know what needs to be done.

HOW TO STRUCTURE YOUR SITE FOR EASY AND AUTOMATIC SEO.

These best practices will ensure your site is structured for better recognition by Google and other search engines.

1. Search engine-friendly URLs.

Have you ever visited a web page and the URL looked something like this:

https://www.examplesite.com/~articlepage21/post-entry321.asp?q=3

What a mess!

These kinds of URLs are a quick way to confuse search engines and site visitors. Clean URLs are more logical, user-friendly and search engine friendly.

Here is an example of a clean URL:

https://www.examplesite.com/football-jerseys

Much better.

Take a quick look at Google's search engine results. You will see a very large portion of sites in the top 10 have clean and readable URLs like the above example. And by a very large portion... I mean the vast majority.

Most site content management systems have search engine-friendly URLs built into the site. It is often a matter of simply enabling the option in your site settings. If your site doesn't have search engine-friendly URLs, it's time for a friendly chat with your web developer to fix this up.

2. Internal navigation

There is no limit on how to structure the navigation of your site. This can be a blessing or a curse.

Some people force visitors to watch an animation or intro before they can access the site. And in the process, making it hard for visitors, and confusing for search engines, to reach the genuine content on the site.

Other sites keep it simple by having a menu running along the top of the site or down the left-hand side of the browser window. This has pretty much become an industry standard for most sites.

By following this standard, you make it significantly easier for visitors and search engines to understand your site. If you intend to break this convention, you must understand it is likely you will make it harder for search engines to pick up all of the pages on your site.

As a general rule, making it easier for users makes it easier for Google.

Above all else, your website navigation must be made of real text links, not images.

If your main site navigation is currently made up of images, call your web designer and change them to text now! If you do not have the main navigation featured in the text, your internal pages will almost be invisible to Google and other search engines.

For an additional SEO boost, include links to pages you want visible to search engines and visitors on the home page.

By placing links specifically on the home page, Google's search engine spider can come along to your site and quickly understand which pages on your site are important and worth including in the search results.

HOW TO MAKE GOOGLE PICK UP THE KEYWORDS YOU WANT.

Many misconceptions are being circulated about what to do, and what not to do when it comes to optimizing keywords on your page.

Some bloggers are going so far as telling their readers to not put keywords in the content of targeted pages at all. These bloggers—I'm not naming names—do have the best intentions and have taken the worry about Google's spam detection to the next level. But it is madness.

Not having keywords on your page makes it difficult for Google to match your page with the keyword you want to rank for. If Google completely devalued having keywords on the page, Google would be a crappy search engine.

Think about it. If you search for "Ford Mustang 65 Auto Parts" and arrive on pages without those words on the page at all, it's highly unlikely you've found what you're looking for.

Google needs to see the keywords on your page, and these keywords must be visible to your users. The easy approach is to either create content around your keyword or naturally weave your keyword into the page. I'm not saying your page should look like the following example.

"Welcome to the NFL jersey store. Here we have NFL jerseys galore, with a wide range of NFL jerseys including women's NFL jerseys, men's NFL jerseys, children's NFL jerseys, and much, much more."

This approach may have worked 20 years ago, but not now. The keyword should appear naturally on your page. Any attempts to go bonkers with your keywords will look horrible and may set off spam filters in search engines. Use your keyword naturally throughout the content. Repeating your keyword once or twice is more than enough.

It's really that simple.

Next up, you need to ensure you have a handful of contextually related keywords on your page. Contextually related keywords are otherwise known as LSI keywords or TF-IDF keywords. Google believes a page is more naturally written and is more extensive if it includes relevant keywords in addition to your main keyword.

What do I mean by contextually related? Well, if you're targeting a keyword like, "dentist san francisco", then contextually related keywords are words that should naturally appear on a page that extensively covers that topic, words like "dentist", "root canal", "dental checkup", "dental procedure", "teeth", "california", and so on.

To successfully optimize a page, you need to have your main keywords and contextually related keywords on the page. Find five or six contextually related keywords and make sure they're naturally covered in your content. LSIGraph and SurferSEO are two great tools for finding keywords Google could consider contextually related to your main keywords.

LSIGraph
https://lsigraph.com/

SurferSEO
https://surferseo.com/

Areas you can weave keywords into the page include:
- Meta description and meta title tags.
- Navigation anchor text.
- Navigation anchor title tags.
- Headings (h1, h2, h3, and h4 tags).
- Content text.
- Bolded and italicized text.
- Internal links in the content.
- Image filename, image alt tag, and image title tag.
- Video filename, video title.

HOW TO GET MORE PEOPLE CLICKING ON YOUR RANKINGS IN GOOGLE.

Meta tags have been widely misunderstood as mysterious pieces of code SEO professionals mess around with, and "the secret" to attaining top rankings. This couldn't be further from the truth.

The function of meta tags is quite simple. Meta tags are bits of code on your site that control how your site appears in Google.

If you don't fill out your meta tags, Google will automatically use text from your site to create your search listing. This is exactly what you don't want Google to do, otherwise, it can end up looking like gibberish! Fill out these tags correctly, and you can increase the number of people clicking on your site in the search engine results.

Below is an example of the meta tag code.

<title>Paul's NFL Jerseys</title>
<meta description="Buy NFL jerseys online. Wide range of colors and sizes. Free delivery and free returns. We accept international orders!"/>
<meta name="robots" content="noodp, noydir"/>

Below is an example of how a page with the above meta tag should appear as a search engine result in Google:

Paul's NFL Jerseys
Buy Paul's NFL jerseys online. Wide range of colors and sizes. Free delivery and free returns. We accept international orders!
https://www.yoursite.com/

Pretty simple, huh?

The title tag has a character limit of roughly 55-60 characters in Google. Use any more than 55-60 characters and Google will likely truncate your title tag in the search engine results.

The meta description tag has a character limit of roughly 155-160 characters. Just like the title tag, Google will shorten your listing if it has any more than 155-160 characters in the tag.

The last meta robots tag indicates to Google you want to control how your listing appears in the search results. It's good to include this, while unlikely, it's possible Google can ignore your tags and instead use those listed on other directories such as the Open Directory Project and the Yahoo Directory.

To change these tags on your site you have three options:

1. Use the software your site is built on. Most content management systems have the option to change these tags. If it doesn't, you may need to install an SEO plugin to change these tags.

2. Speak with your web designer or web developer to manually change your meta tags for you.

3. If you are a tech-savvy person and familiar with HTML, you can change the tags in the code yourself.

LOAD SPEED—GOOGLE MAGIC DUST.

How fast (or slow) your site loads is a strong factor Google considers when deciding how it should rank your pages in the search results.

Google's former head of web spam, Matt Cutts, publicly admitted fast load speed is a positive ranking factor. And later, Google publicly acknowledged load speed is important when announcing their new ranking factors titled the Core Web Vitals (covered later in this book).

If your site is as slow as a dead snail, then it's likely your site is not living up to its potential in the search engines and is disappointing customers. This means improving your site's load speed is an opportunity for an easy SEO boost.

And not only is load speed important for achieving top rankings in Google, but extensive industry reports have also shown for each second shaved off a site, there is an average increase of 7% to the site conversion rate. In other words, the faster your site loads, the more people you will have completing a sale or filling out an inquiry form. Simply put, load speed is not an aspect of your site to overlook.

Every site is built differently, with an endless variation of server configurations, which means improving your load speed isn't as simple as following a checklist. However, the following techniques will work on most sites.

Common load speed improvements.

1. Host your site in the city where your customers reside and load speeds will increase.
2. Alternatively, use a CDN (content delivery network) to host your site on servers all over the world. Visitors will get super-fast load speeds regardless of location. Popular CDN services include CloudFlare and Amazon CloudFront.
3. Enable load speed technologies like caching, compression, minification, and HTTP/2. Most platforms have plugins for this, e.g. W3 Total Cache is a popular plugin offering most of these features on WordPress.
4. Find large files on your site and shrink them. Use software like Adobe Photoshop and you can compress image file sizes from 3MB down to 250KB without visual loss in quality, by using Photoshop's "save for web" feature. An easy win for image-heavy sites.

The above are just a handful of the infinite possibilities for improving a site's load speed. Fortunately, several tools are making it easy to identify speed improvements, and speed bottlenecks, irrespective of the technology your site is built on.

Load speed analysis tools.

1. Google Page Speed Insights
https://pagespeed.web.dev/

Google's great free tool, Page Speed Insights, will give you a page load score out of 100. You can see how well your load speed compares to other sites. You can also see how well your site loads on mobile and desktop. Scores closer to 100 are near perfect.

After running a test on your site, the tool will give you a list of high-priority, medium-priority, and low-priority areas for improvement. You can forward these to your developer to speed up your site, or if you are a bit of a tech-head, you can have a crack at fixing these up yourself.

2. GTmetrix
https://gtmetrix.com/

Gtmetrix is the cream of the crop when it comes to load speed tools, providing detailed breakdowns of files and resources slowing your site down, listing file sizes of individual files, server load times, and much more. It goes into greater depth than the other tools, though probably best suited for a web developer or someone with a basic level of experience building websites.

Large images are easy targets for load speed improvements. If you have any images over 200kb, these can usually be compressed in Photoshop and shrunk down to a fraction of the size without any quality loss. Take note of any large files, send them to your web developer or web designer, and ask them to compress the files to a smaller file size.

3. Lighthouse – Tools For Web Developers – Google
https://developer.chrome.com/docs/lighthouse/overvie
w/

For advanced developers working on complicated projects or sites—i.e. programmers who know what a Node module is—Google released a powerful Chrome extension called Lighthouse. Lighthouse provides reports on website performance, accessibility, adherence to programming best practices, SEO, and more—with actionable steps on improving each of these areas. While owners of basic websites probably won't get additional insights from this tool, on top of recommendations provided by earlier tools, programming ninjas looking for a well-rounded tool to enhance their performance chops will find Google's Lighthouse is the Swiss Army knife of site performance analysis.

THE USUAL SUSPECTS—SITEMAPS.XML AND ROBOTS.TXT.

Sitemaps.xml

Search engines automatically look for a special file on each site called the sitemaps.xml file. Having this file on your site is a must for making it easy for search engines to discover pages on your site. Sitemaps are essentially a giant map of all of the pages on your site. Fortunately, creating this file and getting it on your site is a straightforward process.

Most CMS systems have a sitemap file automatically generated. This includes systems like WordPress, Magento, and Shopify. If this is not the case on your site, you may need to install a plugin or use the free XML Sitemaps Generator tool. The XML Sitemaps Generator will automatically create a sitemaps.xml file for you.

XML Sitemaps Generator
https://www.xml-sitemaps.com/

Next, ask your web developer or web designer to upload it into the main directory of your site or do it yourself if you have FTP access. Once uploaded, the file should be publicly accessible with an address like the below example:

https://www.yoursite.com/sitemaps.xml

Once you have done this, you should submit your sitemap to the Google Search Console account for your site.

If you don't have a Google Search Console account, the following article by Google gives simple instructions for web developers or web designers to set this up.

Add a website property – Search Console Help
https://support.google.com/webmasters/answer/34592

Login to your account and click on your site. Under "site configuration" click "sitemaps" and submit your sitemap.

Robots.txt

Another must-have for every site is a robots.txt file. This should sit in the same place as your sitemaps.xml file. The address to this file should look the same as the example below:

http://www.yoursite.com/robots.txt

The robots.txt file is a simple file that exists so you can tell the areas of your site you *don't* want Google to list in the search engine results.

While there is no boost from having a robots.txt file on your site, it's essential to check you don't have a robots.txt file blocking areas of your site you want search engines to find.

The robots.txt file is just a plain text document, its contents should look something like the below example:

robots.txt - a good example

```
User-agent: *
Disallow: /admin
User-agent: *
Disallow: /logs
```

If you want your site to tell search engines to not crawl your site, it should look like the next example. If you *do not* want your entire site blocked, you must make sure it *does not* look like the example below. It is always a good idea to double-check check it is not set up this way, just to be safe.

robots.txt - example blocking the entire site

```
User-agent: *
Disallow: /
```

The forward slash in this example tells search engines their software should not visit the home directory.

To create your robots.txt file, simply create a plain text document with Notepad if you are on Windows, or TextEdit if you are on Mac OS. Make sure the file is saved as a plain text document, and use the "robots.txt good example" as an indication of how it should look. Take care to list any directories you do not want search engines to visit, such as internal folders for staff, admin areas, CMS back-end areas, and so on.

If there aren't any areas you would like to block, you can skip your robots.txt file altogether, but just double check you don't have one blocking important areas of the site like the above example.

DUPLICATE CONTENT—CANONICAL TAGS AND OTHER FUN.

In later chapters, I will describe how Google Panda penalizes sites with duplicate content. Unfortunately, many site content management systems will sometimes automatically create multiple versions of one page.

For example, let's say your site has a product page on socket wrenches, but because of the system your site is built on, the same page can be accessed from multiple URLs from different areas of your site:

http://www.yoursite.com/products.aspx?=23213
http://www.yoursite.com/socket-wrenches
http://www.yoursite.com/tool-kits/socket-wrenches

In the search engine's eyes, this is confusing as hell and multiple versions of the page are considered duplicate content.

To account for this, you should always ensure a special tag is placed on every page of your site, called the canonical tag.

The canonical tag indicates the original version of a web page to search engines. By telling Google the page you consider the "true" version of the page with the tag, you can control which page is listed in the search results.

Choose the most straightforward URL for users, the URL that reads like plain English.

Using the earlier socket wrenches example, by using the tag below, Google would be more likely to display the best version of the page in the search engine results.

```
<link rel="canonical
" href="http://www.yoursite.com/socket-wrenches
"/>
```

As a general rule, include this tag on every page on your site, shortly before the </head> tag in the code.

USABILITY—THE NEW SEO EXPLAINED.

Mobiles and tablets have overtaken desktops in the vicious battle for Internet market share, with mobile devices now making up more than 60% of all traffic. To ensure a great search experience for users, Google gives advantages to sites with great support for users on all devices. As a result, many SEO pundits found you can get an advantage simply by improving your mobile support.

For example, let's say a mobile user is searching for late-night pizza delivery in Los Angeles. One local business has a site with a large number of backlinks but no special support for mobile users, it's difficult for the user to navigate, the layout doesn't automatically fit the screen, and the menu text is small and hard to use on a touch screen.

Another competing local business has low amounts of backlinks, but great support for mobile users. Its design fits perfectly to the screen and has special navigation designed for mobile users, making it easy to use.

In most cases, the second site will now rank higher than the first, for mobile users. This is just one example of how usability can impact your rankings.

While a term like "usability" can seem vague, let's look at practical steps to improve your usability and the SEO strength of your site.

1. Make your site accessible for all devices.

Make your site accessible and easy for all users: desktop, mobile, and tablet. The simple way is to make your site responsive, which means it automatically resizes across all devices and has mobile-friendly navigation for mobile users. Mobile support is covered in more detail later in this chapter, but you can enter your site into the following tool quickly to see if Google registers your site as mobile-friendly.

Mobile friendly Test - Google
https://search.google.com/test/mobile-friendly

2. Increase your content quality.

Gone are the days of hiring a bunch of low-quality writers to bulk out the content on your site. It needs to be proofread and edited, and the more "sticky" you make your content, the better results you will get. If you provide compelling content, users will spend more time on your site and are less likely to bounce back to the search results. Users will also be more likely to share your content. Google will see this and give your rankings a boost.

3. Use clean code on your website.

There's a surprisingly high amount of sites with dodgy code, difficult for both search engines and Internet browsers to read. If there are HTML code errors in your site, which means, if it hasn't been coded according to industry best practices, your design may break when your site is viewed on different browsers, or worse, confuse search engines when they come along and look at your site. Run your site through the below tool and ask your web developer to fix any errors.

Web standards validator
https://validator.w3.org/

4. Take it easy on the popups and advertisements.

Sites with spammy and aggressive ads are often ranked poorly in search results. The SEO gurus have reached no consensus on the number of ads leading to a penalty from Google, so use your common sense. Ensure advertisements don't overshadow your content or occupy the majority of screen real estate.

5. Improve the overall "operability" of your site.

Does your site have slow web hosting or a bunch of broken links and images? Simple technical oversights like these contribute to a poor user experience.

Make sure your site is with a reliable web hosting company and doesn't go down in peak traffic. Even better, make sure your site is hosted on a server in your local city, and this will make it faster for local users.

Next up, chase up any 404 errors with your web developer. 404 errors are errors indicating users are clicking on links in your site and being sent to an empty page. It contributes to a poor user experience in Google's eyes. Fortunately, these errors are easily fixed.

You can find 404 errors on your site by logging into your Google Search Console account, clicking on your site, then clicking on "Crawl" and "Crawl Errors." Here you will find a list of 404 errors. If you click on the error and then click "Linked From" you can find the pages with the broken links. Fix these yourself, or discuss them with your web developer.

Google Search Console
https://search.google.com/search-console/about

If you want external tools to speed up improving your site's usability, I've found the following two resources helpful:

BrowserStack - Free to try, plans start at $29 per month.
https://www.browserstack.com

BrowserStack allows you to test your site on over +20,000 different browsers and devices at once. You can preview how your site works on tablets, mobile devices, and all the different browsers such as Chrome, Firefox, Safari, Internet Explorer, and so on. It helps make sure it displays correctly across many different devices.

Trymata - Free to try, test results start from $333 monthly
https://trymata.com/

Trymata provides videos, audio narration, surveys of users going through your site, and reports on any difficulties they uncover. Usability tests are good for larger projects requiring objective feedback from normal users.

MOBILE SUPPORT—IMPORTANT SEO EXPLAINED IN SIMPLE LANGUAGE.

Whether we like it or not, mobile users are here to stay and Google is driving the mobile revolution. With the largest mobile app store in the world, the largest mobile operating system in the world, and the largest amount of mobile search users, it's safe to say mobile users are a high priority for Google.

If you are not supporting mobile users, it's important to implement mobile support, not just for better search engine results, but for better sales and conversions. Simply put, the majority of your traffic is coming from mobile users. So let's take a look at how to support mobile users.

How to best support mobile users.

If you want to increase support for mobile devices and be more search engine friendly, you have three options:

1. Create a responsive site.

Responsive sites are the cream of the crop when it comes to sites that support both desktop and mobile devices. With responsive sites, both mobile and desktop users see the same pages and same content, and everything is automatically sized to fit the screen. It's also becoming more common for WordPress templates and new sites to feature a responsive layout.

2. Dynamically serve different content to mobile and desktop users.

You can ask your web developer to detect which devices are accessing your site and automatically deliver a different version of your site catered to the device. This is a complicated setup, better suited for large sites with thousands of pages, with complicated infrastructure, when a responsive approach is not possible.

3. Host your mobile content on a separate subdomain, e.g. m.yoursite.com

While Google stated this implementation is supported, I recommend against it. You need a lot of redirects in place and must jump through giant hoops to ensure search engines recognize your special mobile subdomain as a copy of your main site. Responsive sites are popular for good reason: it's easier and cheaper to maintain one site, than both maintaining a desktop copy of your site and a separate mobile copy of your site on a mobile subdomain.

Improving performance in the mobile search results.

Google stated mobile support is straightforward, either your site supports mobile devices or it doesn't... Well, it's not straightforward. You can get an edge over competitors by using a handful of tools to improve your mobile usability and make your site faster for mobile users.

Run your site through Google's Mobile-Friendly Test Tool to confirm if you support mobile users, use Google's "Test Your Mobile Speed and Performance" tool for actionable steps to speed up your mobile site, and review the Mobile Usability report in Google Search Console and check for any errors worth fixing—and if you're lazy like me, delegate. Send the reports and errors over to your web developer and get them fixed. Who doesn't like a competitive advantage? Work through these tools, make your mobile support better than competitors, and you will crush it in the search results.

Mobile Friendly Test Tool
https://search.google.com/test/mobile-friendly

Google PageSpeed Insights
https://pagespeed.web.dev/

Mobile Usability – Google Search Console
https://www.google.com/webmasters/tools/mobile-usability

The technical details of building a responsive site are beyond the scope of this book and could fill an entire book. In fact, it does, I counted close to 17 responsive web design books on Amazon as I wrote this paragraph... That said, mobile SEO can be ridiculously simple.

If you have a responsive site that delivers the same content to mobile and desktop users, automatically resizes content to the screen, and is fast and user-friendly, all you have to do is follow the SEO recommendations in this book, and your mobile results will be top-notch from an SEO perspective. Alternatively, follow one of the recommended implementations discussed earlier in this section.

For guidelines, direct from the horse's mouth so to speak, you can read Google's mobile support documentation for webmasters and web developers.

Mobile Friendly Sites – Google Developers
https://developers.google.com/search/mobile-sites/get-started

GOOGLE'S SEARCH QUALITY GUIDELINES — AND HOW TO USE THEM TO YOUR ADVANTAGE.

Search quality is an increasingly popular topic in the blogosphere because it can have a massive impact on rankings. Why is this so? Making sure users are sent to high-quality and trustworthy search results is critical for Google to safeguard its position as providing the best all-round search experience.

While this sounds a little vague, you can use Google's search quality guidelines to your advantage and get an edge over competitors. Did you know that Google's search quality team published their "Search Quality Evaluator Guidelines" publicly? If you didn't, now you do.

The document's 160 pages long, so presuming you don't consider a whitepaper leisurely reading, I'll list the most important and actionable takeaways, so you can use them to your advantage.

Google Search Quality Evaluator Guidelines - Most Important Factors

Google's whitepaper lists the holy trio of most important factors when it comes to search quality. And here it is...

EAT... That's right, E.A.T. Expertise, Authority, and Trust. Acronym choice aside, to establish quality, Google is looking at the expertise, authority, and trustworthiness of the website. This includes things like the content quality, the reputation of the site and its authors, publicly-listed information about site ownership, contact details, and several other factors.

Now we know what's important from a top-level perspective, let's zoom into actionable and practical takeaways that will affect the average Joe trying to nudge his way up the search results.

Search Quality Evaluator Guidelines — Key Takeaways

1. Real name, company name, and contact information listed on an about page. If you don't have this information listed on your website, why should Google, or anyone else for that matter, trust you? Better make sure you include it.

2. Excessive and unnatural internal structural links across sidebars and footers. If you've got 150 links in your footer, it's obvious to Google you're trying to do something sneaky, so be conservative with the footer and sidebar links. Keep it restricted to the most important pages on your site or what's useful for your users.

3. Over monetization of content. Specifically, if you are disguising advertisements as the main content or your advertisements occupy more real estate than the main content, then one of Google's search evaluators will probably flag your site as spam. Take a common-sense approach with your ads, don't overdo it!

4. List editors & contributors. Are you publishing a bunch of articles under pseudonyms or generic usernames? Listing editors and contributors, i.e. real people, is more trustworthy and will increase the perceived quality of your page.

5. Provide sources. Publishing generic articles en masse without any reputable sources? You'll get a better-quality assessment, and a higher ranking if you list sources for your articles. Listing sources shows the writer has performed diligence in their research and increases the credibility of the page.

6. Financial transaction pages. All you drop-shippers and ecommerce retailers out there stand up and take note – pages associated with financial transactions (shopping cart, checkout, product pages, etc.) must link to policy pages for refunds, returns, delivery information, and the terms and conditions of your site. Think about it from the user's perspective, if you are an average Joe shopper thinking about buying something and the page doesn't list any of this information, how safe would you feel checking out?

7. Pages offering financial information must be of the highest quality. Google is stricter with these types of pages, as it falls into the "Your Money or Your Life" category – meaning it could affect the financial well-being of the user. If you're publishing this kind of content, make sure you're doing everything you can to provide high-quality, detailed articles, citing sources, fully disclosing financial relationships, and making it clear what author or company is behind the content.

That sums up the most important takeaways from the Google Search Evaluator Guidelines. If you haven't got them on your site, work 'em in and you'll get a leg up over your competitors, or worse, your rankings could suffer. And if you really, really want to sit down and read through the 162-page whitepaper on page-quality assessment, here it is for your enjoyment.

Search Quality Evaluator Guidelines – Google
https://static.googleusercontent.com/media/guidelines.r aterhub.com/en//searchqualityevaluatorguidelines.pdf

READABILITY — SEO FOR THE FUTURE.

One of the strongest ranking factors has been flying under the radar, overlooked by many SEO professionals in their optimization checklists, leaving a golden opportunity for those that know about it. I'm talking about readability.

Google has been outspoken about readability as an important consideration for webmasters. Google's former head of web spam, Matt Cutts, publicly stated that poorly researched and misspelled content will rank poorly, and clarity should be your focus. And by readability, this means not just avoiding spelling mistakes, but making your content readable for the widest possible audience, with simple language and sentence structures.

Flesch readability surfaced in the Searchmetrics Google ranking factors report, showing a high correlation between high-ranking sites and easy-to-read content. The Searchmetrics rankings report discovered sites appearing in the top 10 showed an average Flesch reading score of 76.00 — content that is fairly easy to read for 13-15-year-old students and up.

It makes sense readability is important for Google. By encouraging search results to have content readable to a wide audience, Google maximizes advertising revenues. If Google was to encourage complicated results that mostly appeal to a smaller demographic, such as post-graduates, it would lower Google's general appeal and its market share.

You can achieve an on-page SEO boost, while increasing your user engagement, by making your content readable to a wide audience. Run your content through a Flesch readability test. It will look at your word and sentence usage, and give you a score on how readable it is. Scores between 90-100 are easily understood by an 11-year-old student, 60-70 are easily understood by 13 to 15-year-old students, and 0-30 are best understood by University graduates.

You can use the free tool below and should aim for a readability score between 60-100. To improve your score, edit your content to use fewer words per sentence, and use words with a smaller number of syllables.

Readability Score
https://readable.com/

HOW TO ACCELERATE TRAFFIC AND RANKINGS WITH CONTENT MARKETING.

One of the most powerful on-page SEO strategies is adding more unique, fresh content to your site. If you consistently add new pages to your site, you are going to receive more traffic. In fact, not only can you increase your traffic, you can receive an *exponential* traffic increase as you publish more content.

It's a no-brainer when you think about it. This is why blogs, publishing, and news-type sites consistently get good results in search engines. More content means more rankings, more visitors, and more sales. Let's look at getting started with improving your traffic by adding fresh content.

1. Post new content on a regular schedule.

If you are going to add new content to your site, you need to decide on a schedule and stick to it. This might seem obvious, but you would be surprised at the large number of businesses that talk about starting a blog and never get around to it. It's the businesses with a regular roster of adding content to their site that see regular increases in search rankings, increases in overall search engine performance, and a growing loyal audience. Without a dedicated roster or schedule, it will never get done.

If you can't create content yourself or don't have a budget to hire a full-time marketing assistant, try hiring a ghostwriter.

Good quality writers can be sourced between $25-$75 US per article and you can regularly churn out fresh content to your heart's content. Textbroker and the Problogger job board are two popular services that can put you in touch with talented writers.

Textbroker
https://www.textbroker.com

ProBlogger Job Board
https://problogger.com/jobs/

2. Leverage your social media accounts.

It almost goes without saying, but you should be leveraging social media to drive traffic to new posts or pages added to your site.

Whenever you post new content, post it across all of your social media accounts. Then post it again in a couple of days and you will expose your content to a different segment of fans. You'll increase your social activity and as a result, get higher rankings.

3. Reach out to bloggers writing roundup posts on your blog's topic.

Bloggers often write roundup posts listing their hottest must-read blogs or articles on a particular topic. Reach out to authors, with a personalized message and links to your best blog posts. Take it to the next level by making it easier for the author to update their post—with a short blog description, image, and link to your social channels. Ensure you have a base level of high-value content to start, then start reaching out to bloggers. You can start seeing links to your blog in a week or two, with enough outreach efforts.

Here's a handful of search queries to find relevant roundup posts and digests of blogs in your industry, replace "keyword" with your blog's topic:

"keyword" blogs you should follow
"keyword" blogs you should read
"keyword" blogs in 2023
"keyword" trends in 2023
"keyword" give their tips in 2023
best   "keyword"   blogs

HTTPS & SSL CERTIFICATES.

Google has publicly admitted site encryption is a positive ranking factor in its algorithm. This means it's a good idea to install an SSL security certificate on your site.

If that isn't motivation enough, Google Chrome shows security warnings to users visiting sites without SSL-enabled. The security notice shows up in Chrome's address bar, stating that the website is "Not Secure", with a strong focus on non-SSL sites containing web forms, and when users visit non-SSL sites in Incognito mode.

If you're wondering what the hell I am talking about, you have seen website encryption in action when you log in to your Internet banking or Gmail account. When you see a padlock at the start of the web address, this means the connection is encrypted and the site owner has installed a security certificate and verified ownership of the site.

Website encryption provides a direct connection between the user and the website server, a bit like a tunnel. Because it's encrypted if anybody tries to eavesdrop on this connection any information intercepted will look like gibberish. The only parties who can read the information are the web server and the user. Pretty neat, huh?

Unfortunately, installing a security certificate isn't enough to get an extra boost to your rankings. There is a migration process required to ensure Google picks up everything correctly.

I've listed basic steps below for upgrading your website without any loss in rankings or SEO juice. But this process is more technically involved than weaving a few keywords into the page, you should read the supporting documentation by Google, ask your developer to do this, and possibly consider using professional SEO help before completing this process.

1. Contact your web host or domain registration provider to install a security certificate. Common fees can range from $50 to $500 per year, depending on the type of certificate.
2. Make sure both HTTPS and HTTP versions of your site continue to run.

3. Upgrade all internal resources and internal links in your HTML code to use relative URLs. This includes references to HTML files, CSS files, Javascript files, images, and all other files referenced in your HTML code. This means instead of referring to internal resources in the website code with an absolute address (e.g. http://www.yourwebsite.com/logo.jpg), it should use a relative address (e.g. ./logo.jpg).

4. Update all of your canonical tags to point to the new HTTPS version of your site.

5. Upload 301 redirects for all HTTP URLs to point to the new HTTPS-secured URLs.

6. Verify the new HTTPS version of your site in a new profile in Google Search Console.

7. Upload an XML sitemap to the new HTTPS Google Search Console profile. This sitemap should include all of the old HTTP pages from your site and the new HTTPS pages. We are submitting the old pages to encourage Google to crawl the old pages and register the redirects.

8. Update all links on your social media accounts and other marketing materials to point to the new URLs.

If you want a downloadable copy of this checklist, the SSL upgrade steps for SEO are covered in the free SEO checklist at the end of the book.

Before working through the SSL upgrade steps, make sure you or your developer read through the support guides by Google on performing this upgrade.

Enabling HTTPS on your servers - Google Developers
https://web.dev/enable-https/

How to move a site – Google Search Central
https://developers.google.com/search/docs/crawling-indexing/site-move-with-url-changes

USER BEHAVIOR OPTIMIZATION—HOW TO USE GOOGLE'S MACHINE LEARNING TECHNOLOGY TO YOUR ADVANTAGE.

Ever heard of Project Pigeon, the top-secret World War 2 U.S. military project for developing missiles guided by pigeons tapping on transparent screens?

Project Pigeon was developed by famous Harvard behavioral psychologist B. F. Skinner in the 1940s, and later decommissioned, because in Skinner's words, "no one would take us seriously." Later, Skinner's more notable work on behavioral analysis was taken seriously, establishing behavioral psychology as a legitimate field of psychology.

How we behave online—tapping on screens—has become a point of focus for Google, with user behavior signals, such as bounce rate, time-on-site, and click-through rate positioned strongly in Google's top 10 ranking factors. Google's machine learning algorithm RankBrain observes these behavior signals, recalculating search results in real time. Fortunately, you can use this to your advantage and get higher rankings with user behavior optimization.

Improving user behavior on your site is no longer a 'nice-to-have'... It's a serious requirement for any SEO practitioner and a powerful technique for anyone who wants to rank in the top 10 results.

Read on for actionable techniques for leveraging Google's machine-learning algorithm to shoot your pages to the top of the rankings faster than a pigeon-guided missile.

Boosting Click-Through Rates.

Your click-through rate (CTR) is the percentage of people who see your search listing and click on it. If more people click on your search result than others, this tells Google your page is appealing to users. Get higher click-through rates with these 7 techniques.

1. Fill out the meta title and meta description tags on your target pages. Unfilled meta tags lead to automatically generated snippets by Google, which generally receive low CTRs. For every page on your site with unfilled meta tags, an SEO technician silently weeps.

2. Make meta tags compelling. Think actionable, descriptive, and specific. Sell your page and make it clear why the user should click on your result instead of competing pages.

3. Use numbers and special characters to stand out. Specific numbers naturally attract higher click-through rates. And special characters such as pipes, em-dashes, and brackets make your rankings more eye-catching, gaining more clicks.

4. Use keywords in URLs. URLs with keywords indicate your page is relevant at a glance, getting automatic clicks.

5. Use short URLs. Both users and Google like short URLs, and so do I. Case closed.

6. Target featured snippets and rich snippets. Rich results can gain up to 30% more clicks. The rich snippets chapter later in this book detail targeting these types of rankings.

7. Improve low-performing pages. Look through your Google Search Console keyword report for keywords with low CTRs. Improve the meta tags and URLs on those pages and make them more click-worthy.

Here's an example of a title tag and URL that has been expertly written to attract clicks:

How to Save Money: 20 Simple Tips | DaveRamsey.com
https://www.daveramsey.com/blog/the-secret-to-saving-money

Boosting Time On Site.

Time-on-site, bounce rates, pages-per-visit... These metrics measure similar things—are users sticking to your content like glue, or are they immediately clicking the back button to find a better result?

How users engage with your content is considered super important by Google's machine learning algo RankBrain, if you can improve your time on site, you can improve your rankings. Let's look at 4 simple techniques for getting users hooked to your content.

1. Increase internal links in your content. Creating relevant internal links within your content encourages users to open up more tabs and browse more pages on your site, 2 to 3 internal links per blog post is enough without becoming annoying.

2. Make your content readable. Use large font sizes, preferably 16px-18px so people don't need to fetch the magnifying glass to read your content. Use short and simple words. And break your content down into subheadings, numbered lists, short paragraphs, and sentences.

3. Use longer word counts. It stands to reason it takes longer for users to read long articles. And according to a study by Ahrefs, content with longer word counts attract more links automatically. Nice.

4. Use videos. Video is 65% of all Internet traffic according to several studies. Simply put, Internet users love video. Every user who watches videos on your pages boosts your time-on-site metric in heavenly ways.

5. Use interactive media. Interactive media such as slideshows and online tools are time-tested techniques to boost time on-site and user engagement.

Google's Core Web Vitals.

Ever waited for a slow page to load on your mobile, moved your finger to tap where you want to go—and BAM—an annoying ad appeared under your finger and you've accidentally tapped to a page you never wanted to visit?... Annoying, right? Well, thank goodness Google decided to send the Page Experience Police to put an end to this ghastly behavior.

Google HQ laid out the master plans for the "Page Experience Update", a major update to the algorithm, on the Google Search Central Blog, which confirmed three new signals into Google's algorithm known as the "Core Web Vitals", which measure a user's experience when they visit your page.

Google announcing a change to the algorithm is rare. It's time to sit up and pay attention when this happens. It is something that will affect all websites and is an opportunity to get an easy rankings boost.

These ranking factors focus on mobile and desktop. So when working through your site, make sure these areas are improved for both mobile and desktop users, and you'll be two steps ahead of competitors. Read on for details on taking advantage of the web vitals to boost your rankings.

What are the Core Web Vitals?

The Core Web Vitals are three metrics that measure how positive (or how annoying) a user's experience is. Here they are:

- Loading. How long it takes for most of your content to load?
- Interactivity. How long it takes for the page to respond to user interactions?
- Visual Stability. How visually stable your page is while loading—does everything stay in the same place or does it look like a popcorn machine about to explode?

How to Improve the Core Web Vitals.

If you're a technical newbie, there's some tech jargon ahead. Forward the links to your tech team or developer, ask them to improve the following areas, then skip on to the next section. This is a technical update and there's no way around it. Just ask for screenshots of the performance, before and after any changes, so you can measure results.

If you're a JavaScript ninja or a tech junkie like myself, read on for easy wins for improving the 3 vitals, tools for measuring the 3 vitals, and official documentation from the smart lads at Google.

1. Improving Loading.

The first Core Web Vital, Largest Contentful Paint, is all about making your main content show up faster. Having your Largest Contentful Paint occur within 2.5 seconds is a good range according to Google's guidelines. Fixing the following easy wins should be more than enough to make your content load blazingly fast, but if you want to do a deep dive, read the developer's guide below.

- Slow server response times.
- Optimize your server.
- Route users to a nearby CDN.
- Cache assets.
- Serve HTML pages cache-first.
- Establish third-party connections early.

Optimizing Largest Contentful Paint - Web.Dev
https://web.dev/optimize-lcp/

2. Improving Interactivity.

The second Core Web Vital, First Input Delay, is all about how fast your page responds to user input. Overall, the biggest cause for slow responsiveness is heavy JavaScript clogging up the page. Ensuring your pages respond to user interactions within 100 milliseconds is a good range, according to Google's technical guide. The following easy wins will speed up page responsiveness, if you want more juicy details, then check out the developer's guide below.

- Break up Long Tasks.
- Optimize your page for interaction readiness.

- Use a web worker.
- Reduce JavaScript execution time.

Optimize First Input Delay - Web.Dev
https://web.dev/optimize-fid/

3. Improving Visual Stability.

The third Core Web Vital, Cumulative Layout Shift, is all about how much your page bounces around while loading, less is better (well, duh!). Making sure less than 10% of your layout shifts while loading is a good goal, according to Google's guidelines. Fix the following low-hanging fruit and your page will be visually stable while it loads. If you still experience issues, read the following technical documentation.

- Images without dimensions.
- Ads, embeds, and iframes without dimensions.
- Dynamically injected content.
- Web Fonts causing flashes of invisible or unstyled text.
- Actions waiting for a network response before updating DOM.

Optimize Cumulative Layout Shift - Web.Dev
https://web.dev/optimize-cls/

Core Web Vitals Tools.

The following tools will help you measure the Core Web Vitals on your website, find opportunities to improve them, and track results.

Chrome Web Vitals – Google Chrome Extension
https://github.com/GoogleChrome/web-vitals-extension

Core Web Vitals Report – Google Search Console
https://support.google.com/webmasters/answer/920552
0

Lighthouse – Google Chrome
https://github.com/GoogleChrome/lighthouse

Core Web Vitals Resources.

Again, if you're not very technical, don't be overwhelmed, forward the above links to your web developer, the three areas of improvement are easily fixed on most sites. If you're a developer or technical person like myself, the above easy-wins are more than enough to ensure the Core Web Vitals are performing well on the majority of websites. For the detail-a-holics out there wanting all the official details from Google HQ, check out the links below.

Evaluating Page Experience For a Better Web – Google Search Central
https://developers.google.com/search/blog/2020/05/evaluating-page-experience

Learn Web Vitals
https://web.dev/learn-core-web-vitals/

~

That sums it up for the on-page SEO chapter.

If you have a small business, the optimization factors mentioned earlier in this chapter are what will make a difference—such as ensuring your site has the right keywords and is accessible to all users.

If you are doing SEO for a large company and need a large amount of traffic, regularly publishing new content and ensuring structural areas of your site are set up correctly, are strategies that will make a difference—such as regularly posting new blog posts, ensuring you have sitemaps working correctly, and no duplicate content or 404 errors.

What's most important is you act. On-page SEO is often the easiest part of SEO. The power is in your hands to fix these areas on your site. Remember small changes can lead to big results. Put these methods to practice and start improving your rankings.

Just like the keyword research steps, for readers who want to put the theory into practice, all on-page optimization tips from this chapter are included in the SEO checklist. I recommend finishing the book before downloading the checklist and the on-page SEO steps, so you are familiar with the theory behind the practical steps.

4. LINK BUILDING. HOW TO RANK EXTREMELY HIGH ON GOOGLE.

WHY IS LINK-BUILDING SO IMPORTANT?

The previous chapter described how to make your site more visible to search engines with on-page SEO. But if you want to show up at the top of the search results your site needs links.

You may have wondered what makes links so important, especially when there are so many factors Google uses to rank sites. The truth is, links are such a strong factor, it is unlikely you will rank high for a keyword if you are competing against sites with more backlinks.

When you think about it, links are the currency of the web. Each time a page links to another, it is a vote for the value of the page being linked to. If a page provides massive value to Internet users, it stands to reason it will get links from other websites. This is why links are such a strong factor in Google's algorithm.

Link building is the key to ranking your site high in search engine results.

THE DIRTY LITTLE SECRET NO ONE WANTS TO TELL YOU ABOUT LINK BUILDING.

There are a lot of opinions circulating the Internet about the best kind of links to build to your site. So much so, they often escalate into heated discussions.

What is the best link? A link from a government site or a high-trafficked blog? Is it better to get a link from a highly relevant site or a site with a lot of social media activity?

The dirty secret no one wants to tell you about link building is *there is no single best kind of link.*

If this weren't the case, Google wouldn't work. Everyone would go out and find a way to spam their way to the top of the rankings very quickly. Having thousands of one type of link pointing to a page is suspicious and a clear sign the site owner is gaming the system.

That said, as a rule, you should try to build links on authoritative, relevant, and high-quality sites. High-quality, relevant links are much stronger than links from low-quality, unrelated sites.

HOW TO ACQUIRE LINKS AND WHAT TO AVOID IN LINK BUILDING.

Many stories are floating around about business owners being slammed by Google for no good reason. Don't let the horror stories mislead you.

In most cases, what happened is the webmaster was doing something suspicious or outdated, like building thousands of links to their site from link directories, and then their rankings suddenly dropped off from Google's top 10 search results.

If you don't exhibit overly spammy behavior in your link building, as a general rule you will be OK.

These best practices will ensure you acquire links correctly and don't break Google's terms of service:

1. Acquire links naturally and evenly over time. Your links should be attained consistently and organically.

Google has made its approach to assessing link acquisition with time public knowledge. Patent US20050071741 outlines how Google analyzes the age of links and the rate they are acquired and then uses this information to calculate the search results.

If you don't fancy reading up on patents in your spare time, then just remember to gradually build up your links over time, so Google sees that your website is acquiring links organically. Don't go out and buy one thousand links pointing to your site overnight or you're sure to set off a red flag in Google's system and get into its bad books.

2. Don't purchase links unless you know what you are doing. Buying links to boost your rankings is against Google's spam policies and you risk being penalized. These kinds of links may work but are generally not worth the potential damage unless you are confident you know what you are doing.

3. Forget about link-swapping or link-trading. These schemes are completely obvious to Google, and either no longer work or may harm your site. This goes against common knowledge, but I've achieved countless number-one rankings for ridiculously competitive keywords without ever swapping links. Link-swapping is extremely time-consuming and completely unnecessary. Get by without it.

4. Don't spam message boards, article sites, or blog comments with crappy content. This might work temporarily, but strategies such as these are outdated very quickly.

5. There are paid networks out there offering to build new links to your site for a low monthly fee each month. Never use them. These networks are against Google's spam policies and using them is a quick way to ensure you find yourself in hot water with Google.

ANCHOR TEXT. WHAT'S ALL THE FUSS?

There has been some controversy around anchor text, as touched on in a previous chapter. Anchor text is the text contained in a link. Anchor text *was* one of the strongest factors for achieving top rankings.

If you had one thousand links to your site with "NFL football jerseys" as the link text, and competitors only had a handful of links with the same anchor text, it was likely you would rank number one. That is until Google's Penguin update effectively put an end to SEOs using "exact match" anchor text as their strategy. Now it is just simply too risky.

Not only is it no longer as effective as it once was, but building hundreds of "exact match" links to a site actually can prevent it from ranking for that keyword.

So then, you might wonder, what is the best way to build up anchor text?

It should be natural.

It is OK to have your targeted keyword in your anchor text, but it should not be the only keyword or the main keyword in all of your links, and there should be a mix of related keywords.

If you think about it, this is a pattern all legitimate sites naturally attract. It defies logic that a quality site would automatically be linked with the same text throughout the entire World Wide Web.

Look over the below examples to see a bad anchor text profile compared to a natural anchor text profile:

Bad anchor text – text in external links
http://www.examplefootballbrand.com/football-jerseys.html
NFL football jerseys - 200 links

Good anchor text - text in external links
http://www.examplefootballbrand.com/football-jerseys.html
examplefootballbrand - 50 links
NFL football jersey store - 10 links
NFL football jerseys - 5 links
http://www.examplefootballbrand.com - 25 links
football jersey store - 5 links
football jerseys online - 5 links
football jacket store - 15 links
click here - 7 links
website - 15 links

The above good anchor text example illustrates the natural way sites accumulate links over time. Your target keyword should not be the most linked phrase to the page.

You can learn a lot by looking at the search engine results ranking in Google, entering high-ranking sites into Link Explorer, and looking at their anchor text. You'll notice almost every top-ranking page has natural anchor text, like the good example above.

Track your link-building efforts and keep them in a spreadsheet. This way you can monitor your anchor text and make sure it fits in with best practices.

Link Explorer
https://moz.com/link-explorer

SIMPLE TO ADVANCED LINK-BUILDING STRATEGIES.

The link-building strategies below will help you build up quality links pointing to your site, and give Google a nudge to rank your site higher, ranging from simple tactics for the small business, right up to the enterprise-level SEO agency looking to roll out links on a large scale.

Directory links.

Directory links are a tried and true form of link building that received some flack in recent years. This is due to Google penalizing spammers who built ridiculous amounts of low-quality directory links to their sites.

Directory links shouldn't be overlooked. In fact, directory links should be the first place to start with any link-building project. There's a solid amount of high-quality business directories where you can get powerful backlinks with a minimum of effort.

But just to be safe, your directory links should not make up much more than 10-20% of your total links. They must also be relevant and quality sites, i.e. not sites with web addresses like seolinksdirectory.com or freelinksdirectory.com. Sites like these just smell like spam! Before building a link on a directory, ask yourself, "Does this look like a legitimate and trustworthy website?" If the answer is no, then move on and focus on legitimate, quality sites only.

To find relevant directories, use the below search terms in Google, replacing "keyword" with your targeted keyword or industry, and you can find relevant directories for your niche:

keyword + submit
keyword + add URL
keyword + add link
keyword + directory
keyword + resources

Here is a short list of business directories to get started:

https://www.linkedin.com/
https://www.bingplaces.com/
http://www.yelp.com/
https://www.mapquest.com/
https://www.yellowpages.com/
https://www.manta.com/
https://www.local.com/
https://www.citysearch.com/
https://www.merchantcircle.com/

Stealing your competitor's links.

Stealing your competitor's links is an old-school tactic receiving a resurgence in recent times, due to Google's increased focus on links from quality sites, making it more difficult to find easy link opportunities.

If your competitor has done all the heavy lifting, why not take advantage of their hard work? Use the below sites to export your competitors' backlinks. By looking through their links you can often find link opportunities to build links pointing to your site. In most cases, you can be confident you are going after SEO-friendly link sources if the competitor is already ranking well in Google.

Ahrefs - $99 per month.
https://www.ahrefs.com/

Majestic SEO Backlink Checker – Free to try then $49 per month.
https://majestic.com

Moz Link Explorer – Free to try then $99 per month
https://moz.com/link-explorer

Video link building.

Google loves videos, and it especially loves videos from video powerhouse YouTube. Probably because Google owns YouTube... If you want the opportunity to capture visitors from the world's largest video search engine, posting videos will considerably help your SEO.

Post relevant how-to guides, industry news updates, and instructional videos for the best response from users. Then link to the relevant pages on your site in the description.

The key to success in video link building is to ensure the video and your description are related. You should aim to have your targeted keywords on the page somewhere.

And don't worry. Your video doesn't have to be on par with the latest Martin Scorsese masterpiece. It can be a simple 5 or 10-minute video, educating visitors with useful knowledge about your topic. Just focus on making it contribute value for the viewer.

The tools below can help with quickly creating videos and uploading them to the web.

OBS Studio
https://obsproject.com/
OBS Studio is free, open-source screen recording software allowing you to record high-quality screencasts from your computer. You can download video files in high quality after you have finished or make live streams. OBS Studio is free, and works on Windows, Mac, and Linux, but can be a little technical to use. User-friendly alternatives include QuickTime Player's native screen recording function for Mac users or a paid screen recording app like Camtasia.

High-quality sites you can easily visit, upload videos and get backlinks from:

https://www.youtube.com/
https://www.vimeo.com/
https://www.veoh.com/
https://www.dailymotion.com/
https://www.archive.org/

Link bait.

Link bait is a new and effective strategy for building high-quality and powerful links on a large scale. Link bait is great because you create content once, but you can have thousands of people over the Internet sharing and linking to your content, while you sit back and put your feet up.

But what is link bait exactly? Link bait is any kind of compelling content that naturally acquires links from other sites as a result.

While there is an art to creating link bait successfully, you would be surprised how easy it is to earn links and social media activity with this strategy. The key is, your content must be so valuable it would almost be worth paying for.

To create this content, you should use your expertise or hire researchers to put together juicy industry content that lends itself to being shared. If there are already 10 blog posts or whitepapers on the same topic, then you're doing it wrong. Try and make it original, substantial, and useful.

Wrap up this content into a whitepaper, a top 10 list, an easy-to-understand infographic, or a downloadable resource and make it compelling enough for visitors to read and share.

Promote this content heavily through your site and social media accounts. Encourage readers to share the post at the bottom of the content. Make sharing the content as easy as possible and you will maximize results.

Next up, find popular link bait in your industry or niche. Then use a link analysis tool such as Ahrefs or Link Explorer to pull a list of sites linking to the popular content. Send out a quick email blast to site owners and bloggers to let them know about your bigger and much better resource.

If you want to take link baiting to the next level, write and publish a compelling press release about your link bait content. With a press release, it can be exposed to thousands of journalists and potentially has a chance of attracting media coverage.

You might be wondering what a successful link-baiting campaign looks like. I've listed examples below:

WordPress SEO
https://yoast.com/wordpress-seo/
Joost de Valk is well known in the SEO industry, in some part due to his one-page guide to WordPress SEO that is updated every month or so. This guide has earned many links and shares over many years.

101 Motivational Business Quotes
https://www.quicksprout.com/101-motivational-
business-quotes/
This is an excellent example of a great link-bait article that
went viral and could be outsourced for pennies on the
dollar.

Types of link bait:
- Infographics
- How-to guides
- Beginner guides
- Breaking news
- Top 10 lists
- Industry reports
- Whitepapers

Pictochart -Free to start
https://www.piktochart.com/
Great service for infographic generation, and has an easy
drag-and-drop interface to put infographics together in
minutes.

Prlog
https://www.prlog.org/
Prlog offers entry-level free press release syndication
services, with additional coverage for an added fee.

PRNewswire

https://www.prnewswire.com/

Many PR firms will simply write a press release and then release it to PRNewswire and charge a premium for doing so. Cut out the middleman, write up your press release yourself, and you can get massive PR for a fraction of the cost of hiring a PR agent. Packages start at $545 US and scale up for increased syndication.

Posting guest posts on blogs.

Guest posting has become standard practice for many link builders, for its effectiveness in getting high-quality, highly relevant, and contextual links — the type of links Google loves.

Finding guest post opportunities is fairly straightforward. Simply do a few Google searches with the following search terms and you'll find some quality placements. This strategy does require that you or your writer produce articles with a reasonable standard of quality... Articles that are well-written, researched, articulated, and preferably citing sources, are more likely to get social shares and high user engagement — which will increase the strength of the links. Further, if you have a reasonably sized social platform behind you — the editor or site owner might be more enticed to post your blog post.

On the other hand, if you try this strategy on a large scale with cheap, poorly written outsourced articles with bad grammar, providing little benefit for users, it's possible you could harm your rankings. Quality is critical for a successful guest posting strategy.

Try the following search queries in Google, replacing "keyword" with your industry, niche, or topic, for finding guest post opportunities. And use the Google Chrome extension, Link Clump, to copy and paste the search results into a spreadsheet, so you can reach out to the blogs for a guest post placement—which will be covered later in this chapter.

keyword "guest post"
keyword "guest article"
keyword "guest author"
keyword "guest contributor"
keyword "contributor"
keyword "sponsored post"
keyword "write for us"
keyword intitle:"write for us"
keyword inurl:"write-for-us"
keyword "guest post guidelines"

Experiment with it and come up with your own search terms!

Broken link building.

Broken link building is a new, but effective strategy. With this new strategy, you can reach out to quality sites with broken links on their pages, and use this as an opportunity to convince the site administrator to provide an updated link to your site.

When you find a broken link, let them know the broken link exists and that you have an alternative resource on your site that will benefit their readers. With this strategy, you should create a linkable resource on your site. This makes it very easy for the webmaster to point the link to your replacement.

Use the search phrases below to find potential pages with broken links, adding your keyword to the start of the search phrase:

keyword useful links
keyword useful resources
keyword useful sites
keyword recommended links
keyword recommended resources
keyword recommended sites
keyword suggested links
keyword suggested resources
keyword suggested sites
keyword more links
keyword more resources
keyword more sites
keyword related links
keyword related resources
keyword related sites

If you want to automate this process, the service below will do the heavy lifting and tells you which broken links exist on any page you enter into the tool.

Broken Link Checker – Ahrefs
https://ahrefs.com/broken-link-checker

Broken brand mentions.

Broken brand mentions are a fast, simple, and reliable form of link building you can use for almost every SEO project. It goes like this: in some cases when someone mentions your brand they forget to post a link. Track mentions of your brand, and where suitable, reach out and ask for a link back to your site. Use the below tools to track mentions of your brand. If you see a mention of your brand without a link, send a quick email to the author, and they will often be happy to link to your site.

Brand monitoring sites I've found useful:

Google Alerts - Free
https://www.google.com/alerts
Google Alerts is a very powerful brand monitoring tool. Get email alerts whenever your brand name is mentioned, or, when any keyword is mentioned across the web. Both are free and powerful, making them worth checking out.

Mention - Free to try, pricing starts at $49 per month.
https://mention.com/en/
Mention is a powerful brand-monitoring tool that will send an email alert when your brand is mentioned online, so you can respond quickly.

Paid links.

While paid links are against Google's terms of service, these below link-building tactics do work and can fly under the radar. Needless to say, if you're feeling daring, you've been warned and I take no responsibility for what happens as a result of paid link strategies.

Donate to charities & non-profits.

Charities and non-profit sites often have a donors' page. Search for "site:.org + donors" or "site:.org + sponsors" in Google for a list of organizations that have these pages, offer a donation, and request a listing on the page.

Better Business Bureau.

Links from the Better Business Bureau are among the best links you can receive. Better Business Bureau links will pass authority and trust. Check your listing to see if you are already linking back to your site, and if you're not already a member, then consider signing up.

LINK OUTREACH—SCALING UP HIGH-QUALITY LINK-BUILDING CAMPAIGNS.

Link outreach is a common and powerful link technique in use by SEO professionals these days, and for good reason—it's an effective way to scale your high-quality and relevant links.

What to avoid with link outreach campaigns.

Before we jump into link outreach techniques, Google publicly stated guidelines on this practice and it's important to know what to avoid, so you don't get into Google's naughty book.

Here's a direct quote of the combination of factors Google considers bad practice, as discussed in guidelines about large-scale article campaigns:

- Stuffing keyword-rich links to your site in your articles.
- Having the articles published across many different sites; alternatively, having a large number of articles on a few large, different sites.
- Use or hire article writers that aren't knowledgeable about the topics they're writing on.
- Use the same or similar content across these articles; alternatively, duplicate the full content of articles found on your site (in which case use of rel='canonical' and rel='nofollow' tags are advised).

The guidelines are a little vague… The reason being, Google can't completely outlaw guest-posting, nor can it outlaw site owners talking with other site owners to collaborate—that would hardly be fair and an over-reach on Google's part.

Google is mostly concerned the articles are relevant, high-quality, posted on relevant sites, aren't stuffed with extreme numbers of links pointing to your site, and you're not annoying a billion site owners with spammy unpersonalized email blasts filling up their inboxes. Avoid these practices, and you'll avoid getting a slap from Mr. Google.

Here are the official guidelines from the guys over at Google HQ if you want to read up further.

A reminder about links in large-scale article campaigns - Google Search Central Blog
https://developers.google.com/search/blog/2017/05/a-reminder-about-links-in-large-scale

Steps for link outreach campaigns.

Typically, there are two steps for link outreach campaigns:

1. Prospecting - finding link opportunities and finding contact information.
2. Outreach - writing and sending emails, follow-ups, replies, and managing relationships.

We've already covered link opportunities, such as looking through competitors' backlinks and finding guest post opportunities, so let's jump into the nitty gritty of finding contact information and conducting a link outreach campaign.

Finding contact information.

Finding contact information is easy with the right tools. First, you can use a standalone tool for automatically finding contact details on sites while browsing through link opportunities, like Hunter.io's very handy Chrome extension which automatically finds contact details for you, or you can make things simple and try an all-in-one email outreach platform covered in the next section, that both find contact details and sends emails.

Secondly, you should track all your link opportunities in a spreadsheet or Google Doc, and make sure you leave a personal note for each link opportunity, which will later be dynamically inserted into your email (more on this later).

Hunter
https://hunter.io/
Hunter is purely focused on finding contact details and is very good at it. It has a nice Chrome plugin that shows you the contact details it can find for a particular site while browsing. Free plans include up to 100 contact information requests, for more contact requests plans start at $49 per month.

Personalization.

Whichever outreach platform you use, you should always ensure your email is personalized in some way. This includes addressing the author or editor by name, mentioning a recent article that captured your interest, a similarity between your sites, or how you have a particular resource or topic that aligns with something the site owner is passionate about. Leave a note of this in your spreadsheet while reviewing opportunities...

Remember, there's a big difference between contacting a site owner with a relevant, personalized email and mutually-beneficial opportunity for collaboration, and a big spammy email blast to a thousand site owners using the same email template — which could quickly get you in hot water with Google. Don't skip the personalization.

Outreach platforms and scheduling emails.

There's a growing number of outreach platforms due to the increasing popularity of this technique. Here are some popular options on the market. Some only send emails, while others offer end-to-end outreach campaign management, including finding prospects, contact details, sending emails, automated follow-ups, and the whole kit and caboodle. Anyways, here they are.

Mailshake

https://mailshake.com/

Mailshake is pure-outreach. You will need to provide contact information yourself. It is very effective at sending personalized email campaigns, and you can import personalization info including name, address, and a personal message via a CSV file. Includes automatic follow-ups, email template libraries, and more. Plans start at $59 per month.

Buzzstream.

https://www.buzzstream.com/

Buzzstream is the darling of many link builders and content marketers. It is an end-to-end outreach platform, meaning it can find contact details, send emails, track relationships, and more. Buzzstream doesn't allow automatic follow-ups nor one-click sending for your campaigns, so a bit of manual work is required to run campaigns through Buzzstream. Plans start at $24 per month.

Ninja Outreach

https://ninjaoutreach.com/

Ninja Outreach is another end-to-end outreach platform, including finding contact details, sending emails, personalization, automatic follow-ups, and more. I have noticed the majority of bloggers on this platform ask for you to pay to contribute to their site, which is a downside in my opinion. Pricing starts at $389 per month.

Pitchbox

https://pitchbox.com/

Pitchbox is an enterprise-level outreach platform, including finding contact details, personalized emails, automated follow-ups, detailed reporting, and more. Pitchbox is more suited for larger teams or campaigns, SEO agencies, and SEO professionals. It comes at a higher price point, but is sometimes the preferred tool for serious SEO guys and gals, due to having more features and flexibility than the other platforms. Plans start at $550 per month.

HOW TO GET LINKS FROM MAJOR NEWS OUTLETS FOR FREE.

Did you know you can get links from major news outlets such as Fox News, The New York Times, and Time Magazine without paying a cent? Well, you can. The service is called Help A Reporter Out and it connects over 55,000 reporters with sources for news articles every day, for a wide range of topics from cooking tips, small business advice, tech news—you name it. If you've ever wanted badges on your site saying, "featured on Fox News, MSNBC, and CNN", then you've come to the right place.

HARO sends a massive email blast around 3-times every day with reporters' requests for contributors for stories. HARO's emails will flood your inbox, which is why they have paid plans for filtering emails with keywords and SMS alerts. If you're on a budget, no problem, you can use their free plan and only see relevant opportunities by setting up Gmail filters, as described later in this section.

How to get started with HARO step-by-step.

1. Sign up for HARO with the link at the end of this section.
2. Enter your personal information and select the categories you are interested in. It's better to use more categories, we will filter out irrelevant opportunities later.
3. It's a good idea to upload a high-res professional headshot to your website in JPG or PNG format. And if you have one handy, upload a press kit while you're at it (a quick one-pager on the background of your company with contact details for PR professionals). Don't email attachments to reporters or you'll set off antivirus and spam alerts over at HARO HQ and get yourself in hot water. Send links instead.
4. Wait until you start receiving daily emails from HARO. You won't miss it, they will flood your inbox.
5. Follow the instructions in the next section to filter the emails out of your inbox so you're not overwhelmed.

Help A Reporter Out
https://www.helpareporter.com/

Use the "HARO One-Two Punch".

I would like to introduce a technique I call the "HARO One-Two Punch", for maximizing HARO results and keeping your inbox tidy. We're going to create two Gmail filters for HARO emails, one specific and one broad. The specific filter helps you respond to relevant opportunities faster. After you've responded to relevant opportunities with higher success rates, you can respond to broad opportunities to improve your overall media mentions. And best of all, HARO emails will be kept in their own folder, away from your inbox, keeping it all nice and tidy.

Perform the following searches in your Gmail account. Create a Gmail filter for each search, making sure to select "skip the inbox" and "apply label". In the following examples, I've used a Gmail search that would match a travel startup founder based in the San Francisco area. Change the keywords to suit your background.

Example HARO-specific Gmail search - apply the label "haro-specific":
from:(haro@helpareporter.com)
(tech | startup | founder | CEO | travel | San Francisco)

Example HARO broad Gmail search - apply label "haro-broad":
from:(haro@helpareporter.com)   -
(tech | startup | founder | CEO | travel | San Francisco)

See the difference? The minus sign in the second Gmail search hides the specific results from the broad results. If you haven't created Gmail filters before, check out the guide below.

Once set up, make a habit of checking your HARO-specific Gmail folder first, for the most relevant opportunities. Reply to as many relevant opportunities as possible before replying to broad opportunities, to maximize results.

Create Rules to Filter Your Emails - Gmail
https://support.google.com/mail/answer/6579?hl=en

Advanced tips to increase success with HARO.

1. Keep at it. Don't give up on the first or second day. Success rates range between 5%-15%. The more opportunities you reply to, the more you'll be featured.

2. Keep it relevant. Reporters are flooded with responses. If you want to stand out, don't waffle, and don't tell your whole life story. Get straight to the point and answer reporters' questions directly. If you want to provide more background information, provide it after replying to the reporter's questions.

3. Establish your expertise. If you've got it, flaunt it. Reporters want to quote experts. If you are an expert, make it clear in your bio and email signature.

4. Reply to anonymous opportunities. Big publications often send HARO emails with the publication listed anonymously. Why? They don't want to be flooded with irrelevant pitches from small website owners desperate to get a link. Replying to anonymous media opportunities increases your chances of being mentioned in a big publication. It also increases your chances of being featured on smaller and less known sites, a fair trade.

5. Set up Google alerts and get an email alert whenever you're mentioned across the web. More often than not, sources get featured in news articles, sometimes weeks or months later, without even knowing. Fortunately, Google alerts can help you never miss a mention in the media. If you do get mentioned without getting a link, reach out to the reporter or webmaster and ask to have your link included in the article.

Google Alerts
https://www.google.com/alerts

6. Automate your responses with Gmail templates. There's no need to start from scratch every time you write a reply to reporters' questions—we're living in the age of automation, baby! Respond to a few reporters' questions, then save your email as a template in Gmail. Next time, automatically insert your email with just a few clicks, make it customized to the reporter's questions, and get your emails out 10 times faster. To access Gmail templates, click on the more button at the bottom right corner of Gmail's compose window (it looks like three vertical dots). If you can't figure out Gmail's email templates, check out the simple guide below.

Create Email Templates – Google Workspace Learning Center
https://support.google.com/a/users/answer/9308990?hl=en

ADDITIONAL LINK-BUILDING OPPORTUNITIES.

The aforementioned link-building techniques are enough for 99% of readers to push rankings higher than competitors. For link-building junkies who've exhausted the above options, here's a handful of strategies listed in rapid-fire fashion. These are intended for advanced SEO users, who are already actively blogging and building links.

1. Create your own authority links.

The most powerful link-building strategy is to simply go out and make your authority links. By buying a previously owned website or domain, you can turn it into a blog and unlimited source for powerful, highly relevant links for your site.

There are readers out there who will scoff at this strategy and there are readers out there nodding their heads—it's the readers nodding their heads that know how powerful this strategy is. Links from authority sources in your market are much more powerful than any other kind of link, and the easiest way to get authority links is to create your own authority site. Consider buying a website more than three or four years old with a relevant domain, for a more powerful effect.

Be careful with this strategy. If you create a network of sites like this and obscure the ownership details at the domain registry, and only link back to websites you own, you risk being labeled as the owner of a private blog network by Google and could receive ranking penalties. However, if you create a legitimate, authoritative resource creating genuine value for users, you should be fine.

Flippa
https://flippa.com
Marketplace for buying and selling websites.

Sedo
https://sedo.com
Buy and sell domains.

2. Relationship link building.

If you've been following the online advice on blogging and link-building in the past couple of years you will have noticed a recurring theme: building relationships. Building relationships with other bloggers is a powerful way to consistently earn strong backlinks.

While this strategy is only relevant for users with active blogs on their site, fortunately, creating these relationships and getting the links is easier than it sounds. Other bloggers in your industry are just as dependent on links as you are. So why not link to them in your blog posts first? By linking out in your blog posts to other bloggers you 1) give a valuable backlink to the blogger, and 2) give recognition to the blogger for being an authority in the industry. Everyone likes recognition, and the law of reciprocity comes into play here, you will find most bloggers are grateful for being mentioned and happy to link back in a social media post or future blog post.

Try creating or curating popular blog posts into a top-level summary, then send a quick email to the bloggers mentioned, let them know, and very politely ask for a mention or link back. The best part of this strategy is curating blog posts; it is often easier than creating content from scratch.

Example email:
Hey [expert blogger],
Just thought I'd give you a heads-up. I've just featured you in my post [xyz]...
Hope you don't mind. If you're happy with the article, I would appreciate a mention on social media or perhaps a link back. Or if you want anything changed, feel free to let me know.
Really enjoyed your post on [xyz].
Thanks!

An example expert round-up post:

The top marketing trends of 2023 & how they've changed - data from 1000+ global marketers
https://blog.hubspot.com/marketing/marketing-trends

3. Testimonial link building.

An awesome way to get high-quality, relevant links back to your site is to give out testimonials. Sometimes you can earn a link back to your site from somebody else's homepage, possibly one of the strongest types of links! I will sometimes go as far as purchasing a product just to get a testimonial link. Give this strategy a try by finding a few sites with testimonials and offering your own. Of course make it easy for the webmaster by including all the information they need, such as a photo, your name, job title, testimonial and link back to your site. The key is to look for businesses or services with a testimonials page already, or a testimonials carousel or widget on their homepage. Speed up your search with a couple of Google search queries:

"keyword" + testimonials
"keyword" + recommendations
"keyword" + "client testimonials"
"keyword" + "customer testimonials"
"keyword" + "what customers say"
"keyword" + "what people say"

That wraps it up for links. Let's have another look at the techniques we just covered...

- Submitting to business directories.
- Creating videos and creating links in the descriptions.
- Guest posting.
- Broken link building.
- Outreach and asking for links.
- PR and getting featured in news articles with HARO.

- Creating relationships with other bloggers.
- Creating your own authoritative websites for unlimited relevant links.
- Creating testimonials for other products.

Are there more techniques than this? Probably. But they will use the same principles and processes as the techniques we just covered. The techniques covered in this chapter are more than enough to get started and see results. Exhaust these techniques first. Then when you have experience seeing what works and what doesn't, improve the processes and come up with your techniques.

5. SOCIAL MEDIA & SEO.

IS SOCIAL MEDIA IMPORTANT FOR SEO?

Social media has become integral to the way we use the Internet. Important content is not only linked, it is shared, liked, tweeted, and pinned. How people use the Internet has drastically changed, and this hasn't gone unnoticed over at the Googleplex. Many independent studies on Google's ranking algorithm show a large correlation with high-ranking pages having strong social media activity.

While the official stance from Google is that social signals are not directly used in the algorithm, the SEO community pretty much agrees it is certainly a factor in achieving rankings. Disagreements aside, I can tell from my own experience, sites with large social followings consistently get higher rankings in a shorter timeframe.

Not only can you use social media to build social activity to increase your overall SEO strength, but you can also use social media to regularly create backlinks that are free and easy to build. It also increases referral traffic back to your site and engages previous customers. As a rule, social media should be a part of every SEO project, or perhaps every marketing project.

FACEBOOK & SEO.

Facebook is the world's most popular social network. What's popular on Facebook is essentially a snapshot of public opinion, and Google has noted this by making Facebook activity a very strong factor in the algorithm. You should consider using Facebook for every SEO project. If you only have the time or budget to use one social network in your SEO strategy, use Facebook.

To improve your site's Facebook social activity, share content from your site on your Facebook page regularly.

Each time you do this, you receive more exposure from your fan base, and you also build up social activity around the content on your site. Be careful to mix this up with relevant, engaging non-commercial content for your user base, so you don't turn them off and maintain high levels of engagement. Examples include infographics, inspirational quotes, inspirational photos, and so on.

Build up your audience by including a Facebook follow button on your site, your email signatures, and your thank you or success pages.

If you want to speed up building your audience, you can use Facebook advertising to build a relevant audience of loyal customers. This is a good strategy if your competitors in the rankings have a larger following and you are looking to beat them. You can also use Facebook advertising to increase exposure for your posts or run advertising campaigns for a promotional offer. Facebook advertising stands out as a great way to build up an audience, social activity, and referral sales for projects with a budget.

Meta for business
https://www.facebook.com/business

Facebook ads
https://www.facebook.com/business/ads

TWITTER & SEO.

Twitter is filled with discussions on the world's latest news and events. In many cases, groundbreaking news stories are released on Twitter before the world's major news outlets. The death of Osama Bin Laden is the perfect example—it was leaked on Twitter by a former chief of staff to the US Defense Secretary and within minutes it was all over the news.

Google has recognized this and uses Twitter activity in the algorithm. While it may not be as strong as other social networks, you can use Twitter to build up your overall SEO strength. Twitter is a great social network to weave into your SEO strategy as you can schedule a lot of your tweets in advance without coming across as too spammy, and manage your account with only a small commitment of time and effort.

Schedule tweets to your pages such as Hootsuite and start building up your tweet counts on your pages. Mix this up with relevant and informative tweets about your industry. You should aim for a maximum of 12 tweets per day. 12 Tweets per day is roughly the limit you can post without annoying your followers. If you're lazy like me, you can schedule all of your tweets about 3 months in advance.

If you want to encourage site visitors to tweet your content for you, include a "tweet this page" link on every page or blog post on your website.

Tweetdeck -Free
https://tweetdeck.twitter.com/

Free and easy Twitter management software. You can install Tweetdeck on your computer and manage your whole Twitter account from inside the program. Popular features include managing multiple accounts, scheduling tweets, and arranging feeds so you only see updates from Twitterers you're interested in.

Hootsuite -Free to start. $149 monthly for power users. https://www.hootsuite.com/

More advanced than Tweetdeck, you can use Hootsuite to schedule tweets, analyze social media traffic, manage multiple accounts, create social media reports to monitor your success, and much more. Recommended for power users or automating multiple accounts.

OTHER SOCIAL NETWORKS.

Let's face it, we'd all love to play around on social networks all day, but we don't have the spare time to be always looking for great ideas and sharing them endlessly on social media accounts.

If you have limited resources, focus on Facebook, Youtube, and Twitter.

If you are looking for an extra edge, doing SEO for a large brand, or maybe you have an army of helpers waiting for your command, you can gain significant boosts by expanding your social activity to several social media sites.

Set up an account on the below networks, posting on the networks most relevant to your business:

LinkedIn
https://www.linkedin.com/

LinkedIn is Facebook for professionals. LinkedIn is a fantastic networking tool if you are in the business-to-business industry and looking to build up your brand or the brand of your site. If you want to increase your effectiveness on Linkedin, join groups and participate in discussions, post relevant updates about your industry, and post content in the news feed.

Pinterest
https://www.pinterest.com/

Pinterest has become one of the fastest-growing social networks in a very short timeframe. Pinterest's fast-growing user base is primarily made up of women. The site has effectively turned into a giant shopping list of wish-list items. If your target audience is women, you should be on Pinterest.

Instagram
https://www.instagram.com/

Initially, a mobile app to help users make their photos look pretty, Instagram has skyrocketed from a fledgling mobile app to competing with major social networks in just a few years. Instagram limits the number of links you can post, which essentially means the links from your profile on Instagram are much more powerful. If you work in a fashion or image-heavy industry, Instagram is a must-have social network to incorporate into your SEO and overall digital strategy.

SOCIAL MEDIA ANALYTICS.

If you invest time and effort in building up your social media profiles, you will want to track your results so you can separate the parts of your strategy that are successful and not so successful.

Social media analytics are different compared to other web analytics because social analytics are geared toward measuring the conversation and interaction of your fan base with your brand. Using the software listed below, you can monitor results and get valuable insights on how to improve your social media efforts:

Sprout Social - Free for 30 days. $249 per month for regular use.
https://sproutsocial.com/

Sprout Social is a great web analytics and social media management package that allows you to track the performance of your social media profiles over time. It has a free trial, is suited to advanced-level use, and offers powerful analytic reports for major social networks.

Hootsuite - Free plan available. Paid plans start at $149 per month.
https://www.hootsuite.com/platform/analyze

Hootsuite is quoted many times in this book and for good reason — Hootsuite is a robust social media management platform allowing for control over many social networks, as well as powerful web analytics insights. Its paid plans are also quite affordable for pro-users.

Google Analytics Social Tracking - Free
https://marketingplatform.google.com/about/analytics/

Google Analytics' social-tracking features are great for tracking basic social interactions that occur when visitors are on your site. It is free and includes an out-of-the-box solution with the standard setup. To see social reports, log into Google Analytics, click on the "Acquisition" tab in the main menu, then "Social."

6. WEB ANALYTICS IN A NUTSHELL. HOW TO MEASURE YOUR SUCCESS.

Web analytics changed how we do business in the 21st century. Now we can find insights into customers previously impossible to discover, including information on website visitors' demographics, interests, online behaviors, and more. We can find out what works and what doesn't, cut underperforming marketing campaigns, and increase budgets for winning campaigns. Simply put, web analytics have made it easier to grow almost any business. Read on for a quick guide covering the nuts and bolts of web analytics, and how to put web analytics to work for your business.

TRACKING YOUR SEARCH RANKINGS.

With every SEO project, it's important to start tracking how your website appears in the search rankings, for several reasons:

1. Tracking your search rankings measure progress over time and helps you see what works and what doesn't.

2. Tracking search rankings will warn you of potential threats, such as sneaky competitors trying to move into your territory, or Google algorithm updates shaking the search results around.

135

3. If you really want to be tricky, you can track competitors' rankings and get an overview of what they are doing.

Fortunately, tracking search rankings is easier than ever. Most all-in-one SEO platforms already offer rankings tracking with their paid plans, such as Moz and Ahrefs.

All you have to do is copy and paste your keywords into their rankings page listed below, and you're good to go — you can see how high you rank for your keywords in Google, how your rankings perform on both desktop and mobile and measure their movements over time.

When you enter your keywords just make sure you select the correct location, otherwise you could be trying to rank for keywords in New York and tracking search results in San Francisco...

Google Search Console does have reports on search rankings but is not as detailed or customizable as the professional SEO tools. And Google has a history of removing or hiding keyword data from webmasters, for various reasons.

I wouldn't rely on Google Search Console reports alone, unless you're fine to wake up one morning and discover all your data has disappeared because someone at Google HQ decided to change the free reports available to webmasters. Paid SEO tools track keyword rankings for a reason...

SerpWatcher - From $49 Per Month
https://mangools.com/serpwatcher/

Moz Pro Rank Tracking - From $99 Per Month
https://moz.com/products/pro/rank-tracking

Ahrefs - From $99 per month
https://ahrefs.com/rank-tracker

Search Performance Report - Google Search Console
https://search.google.com/search-
console/performance/search-analytics

WHY USE GOOGLE ANALYTICS?

You may have already heard about Google Analytics. Google Analytics is the web analytics platform used by the majority of sites. It has its quirks, but it's the best readily available, all-around analytics tool available for understanding site traffic. And the best part is it's free.

If you don't have Google Analytics installed, put down this book, install Google Analytics now, and then have some harsh words with your web developer. I'm not joking. Without Google Analytics set up, growing a business online is like trying to pilot an airplane blindfolded. Without Google Analytics it's difficult to find out what works and what doesn't, identify issues and solve them before they turn into bigger issues, and get a sense for the general direction your business is headed. Google Analytics is useful for monitoring the performance of a business and applicable to about 95% of businesses.

To get started with Google Analytics, head on over to the below URL and click on "sign in." Create a Google account if you do not have one already, and walk through the simple steps to get started. You may need help from your web developer if you are unable to edit code on your site.

Google Analytics
https://www.google.com/analytics/

HOW TO USE GOOGLE ANALYTICS.

Let me tell you something a little risqué. On its own, most data is useless. You heard correctly, for real awareness and insights, we need to be able to compare data and identify trends over time. There are two ways to analyze and understand data in Google Analytics concerning time:

1. Compare two date ranges.

Click on the date field input in Google Analytics. Enter two timeframes and you can compare them both. Useful date comparisons include comparing this week's performance to last week's performance, last month's performance to the month prior, and last month's performance to the same month of the previous year.

2. Look at the charts over a long time frame.

Simply look at the charts over the longest time period possible and look for trends, without comparing date ranges. This is not so effective for finding hard-to-find information or identifying granular insights, but this approach is useful for a bird's eye view of the direction your traffic is heading.

Note: Seasonality is a factor affecting many businesses. Sometimes you may see a downturn in traffic, but this may not necessarily indicate your site is performing poorly. It could be that your market experiences a downward trend in certain months. If your business is experiencing a downward trend, use the "compare two date ranges" approach and compare the current month's traffic to the same month last year. If you are seeing increases, then you know your site is performing well, irrespective of seasonal trends.

ACQUISITION.

Acquisition is an area of Google Analytics that any business owner or marketer should spend a lot of time reviewing. The Acquisition section of Google Analytics breaks down where your site traffic is coming from. Without keeping a close eye on your traffic sources, it is almost impossible to make informed judgments about the performance of your site or your marketing.

Click "Acquisition" in the main sidebar on the left. In the "All Traffic" section you can see the actual amounts of traffic you've received from a given source. The Channels section listed under "All Traffic" is of special interest. This lists the main sources sending customers to your website. From the "Channels" tab, you can dig further for deeper insights into the performance of specific sources sending customers to your site, such as social visitors, search engine visitors, email visitors, and so on.

ORGANIC SEARCH REPORT.

The Organic Search report is essential for monitoring your performance in search engines. Within the Organic Search report, you can actually see how many times you received a visitor from a search engine.

It's worth mentioning, a few years ago Google made changes to Google Analytics which still has many search engine marketers and marketing professionals shaking their fists at the sky. Early in 2012, Google changed this tool to hide a large portion of the keyword information, making it difficult to get exact information on the keywords customers are using to arrive at your site. Thanks, Google!

Now when someone types a phrase into Google if they are signed into a Google account while browsing, the keyword the visitor searches for will show up as a "not provided" keyword in Google Analytics. When this happens, you have no idea what that person typed into Google before arriving at your site.

The amount of keyword information that has been obscured by Google has gradually increased, but don't be too concerned, we can still measure the overall performance of search engine traffic by looking for total increases or decreases in the Organic Search report.

To view the Organic Search report, click on the Acquisition tab on the left sidebar, click on "Acquisition", "All Traffic", click on "Channels", and click on "Organic Search."

SEGMENTS.

Imagine if you could narrow down to a particular segment of your audience, such as paid traffic, search engine traffic, mobile traffic, iPad users, and so on, and instantly see how many inquiries these users have made, how much time they are spending on your site, what country they are from, and how many sales they are making. This feature exists and it is called Segments

Segments are powerful. With Segments, you can identify portions of your audience that potentially generate more inquiries or sales than other customers. You can also identify portions of your audience having difficulty using your site, and get insights to fix these areas for better performance.

To use Segments, simply click on the "Add Segment" tab at the top of every page and you can choose from the list a large number of Segments for deeper insights.

COMMON WEB ANALYTICS TERMS EXPLAINED.

Pageviews.

A Pageview is counted each time a user loads a page on your site.

Unique Pageviews.

Similar to a Pageview, but if one user loads a page several times it will only be considered one Unique Pageview.

Session.

A session is what occurs when a visitor arrives at the site, and at some point closes the browser. If that visitor returns again, this is counted as an additional session.

User.

If a user visits your site and then returns at a later stage, this is counted as one unique User.

Bounce Rate.

If a visitor visits your site and then leaves without visiting any more pages, this is a bounce. The percentage of visitors who bounce is your bounce rate.

A common question among marketers and business owners is: what is a good bounce rate? There is no general rule. Bounce rates vary greatly between sites and industries. If you find a particular page with a very high bounce rate (+70%), this could be an indicator the visitors do not like the content or they are experiencing technical issues.

Conversion rate.

One of the most important metrics to monitor is your site conversion rate. A conversion rate is the percentage of Users completing a desired action. The action could be filling out an inquiry form, downloading a product, or buying something from you. If you receive one hundred visitors, and three of these visitors complete a sale, this would be a three percent conversion rate.

Goals.

Goals are custom goals you can set up within Google Analytics to track particular business goals or targets you may have for your site.

Common goals to set up include newsletter signups, product downloads, inquiry form completions, and so on.

CALL TRACKING — POWERFUL ANALYTICS FOR EVERY BUSINESS.

Web analytics and VOIP tech have advanced at a lightning pace in the past few years. Tracking and attributing phone calls to marketing channels was previously an arduous task for the local or international marketer, but finally, it's now both cheap and easy to track the source of phone calls in your marketing campaigns.

Better yet, you can track your calls to a great level of detail, including discovering the source of each phone call (Google, Facebook, Google Ads, etc.) and discovering the particular keyword or ad a phone call originated from.

In case you're wondering how this wonderful technology works, most call tracking platforms use a fancy technology called "dynamic number insertion", presenting different phone numbers to different users, depending on where they came from, then tracking it in the platform and presenting the data to you, all neat-and-tidy, on a reports screen or a mobile app.

Before running through popular tools for tracking calls, let's cover important points to safeguard your search engine performance, and make sure you get set up correctly.

Key points for implementing call tracking.

1. If you rely on SEO or local SEO, it's important to keep your "real" phone number displayed on your website, for both search users and Google-bot. Make sure your developer is aware of this, and keep your "real" number displayed at all times to these users in the call-tracking platform. If you don't do this, the "NAP" (Name, Address, Phone number) displayed on your site could become inconsistent, and have a negative impact on search rankings.

2. Make sure the call tracking platform integrates with Google Ads and Google Analytics.

3. If you're using a CRM system, like Salesforce and so on, you might want to check if the call tracking system links up with your particular CRM.

4. Finally, if you're on WordPress or another CMS, ensure the call tracking platform has a plugin for your particular CMS for easy setup. If the platform has a plugin for the software running your site, this often means you can get set up in under an hour or so.

Popular call tracking platforms on the market right now.

Call Rail
https://www.callrail.com/
Call Rail is popular for its ease of use, international support, integrations with Google Analytics, Google Ads, WordPress, and Salesforce, and flexibility. It also includes cool features like text messaging, geo-routing, voicemail, and more.

Call Tracking Metrics
https://www.calltrackingmetrics.com/
Call Tracking Metrics is another popular platform, also offering international support, Google Analytics, Google Ads, WordPress integrations, and overall, similar features to Call Rail. Some online user reports mention preferring Call Rail for its simplicity and flexibility and found Call Tracking Metrics a little difficult to navigate, but in the end, it's often best to trial both platforms initially and see what works best for your business.

OTHER WEB ANALYTICS TOOLS.

There are many web analytics tools out there to help with improving the performance of your site. Google Analytics is great for understanding overall traffic performance, but if you want to delve deeper, check out the following tools for greater insights:

Crazy Egg - Free to start. Plans start at $29 per month.
https://www.crazyegg.com/

If you want a visual indication of how visitors behave on your site once they arrive, Crazy Egg is a fantastic tool. With Crazy Egg, you can get heat maps of where visitors click on the page. You can also see heat maps of how far visitors scroll down the page.

Visual Website Optimizer – 30-day free trial.
https://vwo.com/

Visual Website Optimizer is a popular split-testing analytics tool. With Visual Website Optimizer, you can split-test different variations of your site, and see which version makes more sales or conversions, and increase your overall sales.

Google Tag Assistant
https://get.google.com/tagassistant/

Google Tag Assistant is a handy free tool, for diagnosing any issues with the tracking codes for all the fancy web tracking tools you've set up on your site. It's especially useful for developers diagnosing issues when you're having obvious problems with your web analytics.

Looker Studio by Google
https://lookerstudio.google.com/overview

If you're a data junky then you'll get your fix with Looker Studio. Looker Studio is hardcore, it can create visual reports so you can monitor almost anything—calls, ad campaigns on various platforms, search rankings, Salesforce leads, your bookkeeping system, and the list goes on. The best part is, it's free.

7. TROUBLESHOOTING COMMON SEO PROBLEMS & HOW TO FIX THEM.

Dealing with Google can be massively frustrating at times. Customer support barely exists, and trying to understand why your site isn't playing well with Google can spiral into a wild goose chase.

Don't let Google's lack of customer support or the horror stories dishearten you. Most of the time, if a site is experiencing Google problems, it is only temporary. SEO problems are rarely irrecoverable.

Usually, it's simply a matter of finding out the underlying cause of the problem — more often than not, the cause isn't what the popular blog posts are saying it might be. This sometimes means fixing several items. Once all fixed, you have stacked the deck in your favor and you are more likely to make a speedy recovery.

This chapter outlines common SEO problems that plague website owners.

If you are not at all technically inclined, I urge you to read the section on getting additional advice or consider getting professional help if your site is experiencing serious SEO issues.

WHAT TO DO WHEN YOUR SITE IS NOT LISTED IN GOOGLE AT ALL.

This is a common problem among webmasters and business owners alike.

If you have just launched a brand-new site, it is possible Google has not crawled your site yet. You can do a quick spot check by typing "site:yoursiteaddress.com" into the Google search bar and checking to see if your site comes up at all. If it doesn't, it's possible Google's spider hasn't crawled your site and doesn't know it exists.

Typically, all that's required for Google to pick up your site is to generate a handful of links to your site and some social activity.

Tweeting a link to your site is a quick way to ensure your site is indexed by Google's software, typically within 24 hours. Try to share your site from a handful of social networks for faster results.

Check Google again in 24 hours with the "site:www.yoursite..." search query and see if any pages from your site come up. If you do see pages, this means Google has indexed your site.

If this doesn't work, ask your web designer to set up Google Search Console for you, log in and see if there are any errors. If there are errors, Google will outline the steps to fix them, so Google can see your site.

Google Search Console's handy URL inspection tool is great for troubleshooting and finding issues. It confirms if your page is supported by Google, not suffering from any penalties, successfully appearing in the index, is mobile friendly, and more. To access the URL inspection tool, click "URL inspection" in the left sidebar of Google Search Console.

Google Search Console
https://search.google.com/search-console/about

WHAT TO DO WHEN YOUR BUSINESS IS NOT RANKING FOR YOUR OWN BUSINESS NAME.

A business not coming up in the top position in Google for searches for the official business name is a surprisingly common issue among brand-new sites. Google is smart, but sometimes you need to give Google a nudge to associate your new site with the name of your brand.

This problem is easily fixed by building links to your site, with some of the links using your brand name as the anchor text. This can take up to a couple of weeks for Google to see these links, connect the dots and realize your site is the real deal.

The fast way to get the ball rolling is to do a quick search for the business directories used in your country—Whitepages, Yellow Pages, Yelp, and so on—fill out a listing for your business on each site and include a link back to your web site. The more links the better, but you should be aiming for a minimum of 50 links. In 95% of cases, this will solve the problem of a site not coming up in the top results of searches for the business name.

If this doesn't work, set up Facebook and Twitter accounts for your business, filling out as much information about your business as possible in the profile. Then do a post a day for about two weeks, mixing in links to your site in the posts.

If you still can't get your site ranking high enough, use Link Explorer to spy on competing sites ranking higher for the brand name. Do their pages have more backlinks than the total amount of links to your site? If this is the case, you are going to need to build more links.

WHAT TO DO WHEN YOUR RANKINGS HAVE DROPPED OFF.

Here's a sad truth about SEO: if you achieve a top ranking, it may not keep its position forever. There are billions of web pages competing for top positions in Google. New sites are being created every day. It requires an ongoing effort to keep pages ranking high.

If your rankings have dropped off from the top position and slowly moving their way down the search results, it's possible you've been affected by a Google update or spam filter. Read through the Google Updates chapter later in this book, and also look through the additional resources for keeping updated on new Google updates in the same chapter.

On the other hand, it's more likely your competitors have simply acquired more links or more social activity than your site. Use Link Explorer to spy on competitors, find out how many backlinks they have, and how much social media activity they have, and set these amounts as your target to build your rankings back up.

Next, it's time to start a link-building campaign with the targeted keywords as outlined in the chapter on link-building.

HOW TO SEEK PROFESSIONAL HELP FOR FREE.

Finding the right SEO help can be frustrating for site owners. There is a lot of information to navigate, with varying levels of quality and accuracy. It's difficult to get in touch with SEO practitioners at the top of their field.

That said, there are sites that can put your questions in front of world-leading experts on almost any topic for free. Use the below sites for highly technical responses, and you can create an army of Internet experts to try to solve your problem for you.

The key to success with the following resources is to be specific. The more specific you are, and the more information you provide, you increase your chances you will receive a detailed answer that will point you in the right direction.

For greater results, post your question on *all* of the sites below, and sit back and wait for the answers to come in. You will get more answers and will be in a better position to consider which solution is best.

Moz Q&A
https://moz.com/community/q/

Moz's Q&A forums used to be private, but were eventually recently released to the public. Here you can speak with a large number of SEO professionals directly and attract high-quality answers to your questions. Great for SEO-specific problems.

Pro Webmasters
https://webmasters.stackexchange.com/

The Pro Webmasters Q&A board can have your questions answered by webmasters of high-performing sites.

Quora
https://www.quora.com/

Quora is a Q&A posting board, where you can get a question answered on almost anything. On Quora, questions are sometimes answered by high-profile experts. Marketers, business owners, you name it, there are many leading industry authorities posting answers to questions on Quora.

WordPress Answers
https://wordpress.stackexchange.com/

If your site is built on WordPress, it's inevitable you will eventually encounter some kind of technical hurdle. The WordPress Answers Q&A board is a great resource to seek out help.

8. LOCAL SEO. SEO FOR LOCAL BUSINESSES.

WHY USE LOCAL SEO?

Unless you have been living under a rock, you have seen listings for local businesses appearing at the top of search results in Google and Google Maps. Local listings — previously known as Google+ business pages, then rebranded as Google My Business, now known as Google Business Profile listings — however they will be named next, are a powerful marketing tool for small businesses.

Let's look at some statistics, the following facts were discovered in several recent studies on the behavior of local customers.

- 97% of search engine users have searched online to find a local business.
- 76% of consumers who conducted a local search on their smartphone visited a store within a day.
- 78% of local mobile searches lead to an in-store purchase.
From 12 Local SEO Stats, Every Business Owner and Marketer Should Know – Social Media Today

Holy mackerel, if you are a local business owner and those figures aren't making your jaw drop, I don't know what will. Now that we know if you own a local business, local search can be the Yoko Ono to your John Lennon, let's delve deeper and find out what makes a local search result.

Local search results differ from traditional organic search results by representing a local business instead of a normal web page and appearing at the top of the search results and on map listings.

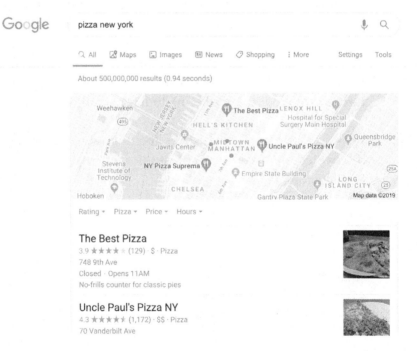

Users can get business contact details, opening hours, and reviews and find the information they need quickly and easily, instead of having to dig around a clunky business site.

Local listings can be a powerful tool to attract traffic. In many cases, local listings can lead to many more inquiries than regular SEO rankings. But does this mean you should scrap traditional SEO in favor of local SEO? Nope. You can do both and potentially double the amount of traffic you can receive.

HOW TO RANK HIGH WITH LOCAL SEO.

Ranking high with local SEO takes a different approach than traditional SEO. Google's algorithm is looking for a different set of signals to determine the popularity of a business, to then decide how to rank it in the search results.

If you think about it, if a restaurant is really popular in a city, a whole bunch of links from all over the world probably isn't the best factor to determine how valuable the business is to the local area.

A better indicator of the importance would be mentions of the business's name and phone number across the web, customer reviews, and details on the website that show the business is based in the area being searched.

The most important factors Google uses for local results are listed below:

- *On-page* optimization (keyword optimization, etc).
- Links (quantity and quality of links).
- Google Business Profile optimization (keyword optimization, profile completeness, photos, videos, etc).
- Reviews (quantity, quality, and positivity)
- Behavioral metrics (time on site, bounce rate, etc).
- Citations (NAP mentions on external sites).
- Personalization (search history, search location, device).

If you want to rank high in the local results, all you have to do is ensure your site and Google My Business page have more of these factors than competitors.

For more detailed breakdowns of the local SEO ranking factors, you can visit the link below.

Brightlocal Local Search Ranking Factors
https://www.brightlocal.com/learn/local-seo/introduction-to-local-seo/ranking-factors/

GETTING STARTED WITH LOCAL SEO.

To get started, the first step is to create your business page on Google My Business. Visit the URL below and complete every area of your profile possible. This means creating a detailed description of your business, available payment methods, and so on. The more information you complete, the more you increase your chances of ranking your page higher.

Google My Business
https://www.google.com/business

When creating your business listing, make sure you choose the most accurate category for your business, e.g. if you provide plumbing as a service, you want to choose "plumbing" as your category, not "trades" or "home repairs."

BUILDING CITATIONS.

Citations are the links of local SEO. A citation occurs each time your name, address, and phone number (NAP) are mentioned on the web. The more citations you have, the more likely your site will rank high. The easiest places to build citations are the many local business directories available for businesses.

While there are many online directories for creating business listings, the following websites would be a good start for a US-based business.

https://www.facebook.com/business
https://www.linkedin.com/
https://www.yellowpages.com/
https://business.yelp.com/
https://www.local.com/
https://www.whitepages.com/business
https://www.manta.com/
http://www.citysearch.com
https://business.foursquare.com/
https://www.merchantcircle.com/

BUILDING REVIEWS.

Citations and reviews are the link-building of local SEO. If you are only building citations, you only have half of the equation covered. To rank high, your business needs to accumulate online reviews.

Many businesses struggle with this. This is because it's tough to get customers to fill out reviews! You have to make it easy.

Include links to your business Google My Business page on your site, email signatures, flyers, and business cards, prompting customers to leave a review. Encourage customers at the end of each sale or transaction to leave a review. By creating every opportunity possible for customers to leave a review, you can significantly increase reviews.

But whatever you do, don't buy reviews. This is a quick way to get into Google's naughty book. Purchased reviews can be picked up by Google's filters and are likely to be excluded from your business profile anyways.

Feeling lazy to hire a graphic designer? No problem! Google created an awesome tool that generates free posters, signs, and stickers to put in your store and encourage more reviews from customers. Check it out at the following URL.

Google My Business Marketing Kit – Think With Google
https://marketingkit.withgoogle.com/

SUPERCHARGING LOCAL SEO WITH PHOTOS AND VIDEOS.

For better or worse, for many people, taking selfies and photos of what they're eating has become a daily habit, and it comes as no surprise Google is capitalizing on this ubiquitous trend.

Google allows video uploads from the general public to Google Business listings on Google Maps—an underused marketing opportunity flying under the radar for now—and savvy local business owners can use this to their advantage.

Why are photos and videos important for a local business?

Whether or not the number of photos and videos uploaded to a Google Business listing is a ranking factor is unknown—it wouldn't be surprising if it is, it would be a solid indicator of the popularity and activity of a local business. But you can be sure Google will stay tight-lipped on the matter. Either way, more photos and videos uploaded to your Google Business page will lead to higher user engagement with your profile, which will likely lead to higher rankings.

But the real advantage lies in enticing more customers to your business through imagery. Ever heard the phrase, "a picture is worth a thousand words?" Customers researching a local restaurant, cafe, or hotel are heavily focused on photos when deciding where to go. Just look at your own experience – ever taken a peek at the photos and videos of a restaurant or hotel, and a particular photo put you over the edge? If you haven't included photos and videos in your local SEO efforts, you're missing out on a piece of the pie. Here are two simple approaches to get amongst the action.

1. Encourage customers to share their experience at your business.

Encouraging customers to share their experience at your business with a photo or video is an effective way to build up authentic photos associated with your page. It'll build up the perceived popularity of your business too. Why not take it to the next level, and entice customers with a free drink or discount on their meal by sharing their experience?

For the general public to upload photos or videos, all they need to do is tap on your listing on Google Maps, scroll down, and click "add a photo", and done! The official guide by Google is listed below.

Add, Remove, or Share Photos and Videos – Google Maps Help
https://support.google.com/maps/answer/2622947

2. Add photos and videos to your business profile.

If you're running a restaurant, hotel, cafe, or any other local-type business for that matter, you should have a handful of professional-looking photos uploaded to your profile at a bare minimum—so customers know what to look forward to when visiting your business, or what they're missing out on...

Fortunately, adding photos and videos to your Google Business profile is easy as pie. Simply log in to Google My Business, click photos on the left menu, and upload away. For additional documentation, check out the official guide from Google HQ below.

Manage photos or videos for your Business Profile - Google My Business Help
https://support.google.com/business/answer/6103862

LOCAL SEO RANKING CHECKLIST & ESSENTIAL RESOURCES.

While looking at your local competitors and working to beat them is probably the best overall strategy, progressing through the following checklist will put you well on your way to ranking high at the top of the local search results.

1. Verify your business profile on Google My Business.
2. Fill out as much information as possible on your Google My Business profile, including description, category associations, images, and videos.

3. Include your business name and location somewhere on your website, this could be your contact page or home page.

4. Include your full business name, address, and phone number somewhere on your site, these should be grouped together so Google will register them as a citation.

5. Include the appropriate schema.org tags in your website markup, following the specification for local businesses at the following URL.

Schema.org Local Business Specifications.

https://schema.org/LocalBusiness

6. Encourage customers to review your business.

7. Submit your website to major business directories like Yelp, Yellow Pages, CitySearch, and so on. You can use tools like Moz Local to submit your business to all of the major directories in one go.

Moz Local.

https://moz.com/local

8. Cross-check your business listings for correct NAP data. These details need to be consistent across your Google My Business listing, website contact page, and external business listings.

A downloadable copy of the above steps is also available in the SEO checklist at the end of the book.

Essential local SEO resources for keeping up to date.

Just like traditional SEO, local SEO constantly changes and becomes more complex over time. To keep your skills sharp you need to stay up to date with the latest knowledge in the industry. The resources below should be considered essential reading for anyone looking to hone their local SEO skill set.

Local SEO Guide
https://www.localseoguide.com/

Andrew Shotland's Local SEO Guide is an enduring commentary on local SEO techniques and updates in the industry. His useful blog has been around for as long as local SEO has been a thing and is popular among the SEO community for good reason—the blog's regular contributions and willingness to give away valuable and actionable advice.

Local SEO News - Brightlocal
https://www.brightlocal.com/blog/

Local SEO News by Brightlocal is a blog that covers all the latest updates and techniques in Local SEO, with lots of useful guides for getting better performance with local SEO and new best practices you should be aware of.

9. HOW TO DOMINATE SEARCH WITH RICH SNIPPETS.

WHAT ARE RICH SNIPPETS?

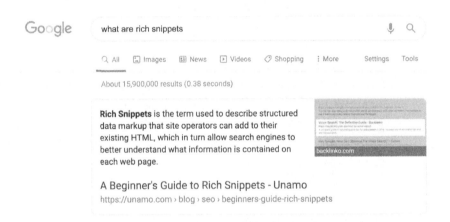

Ever searched in Google and seen a ginormous ranking just above the search results?... These large search results are called "rich snippets" and can send a mind-blowing amount of traffic.

Before I jump into techniques, are you still not sure what I'm talking about? Quickly Google a couple of questions and look for the giant search result at the top of the results, you can't miss it—it's four times bigger than a regular search result. Here are example searches that usually deliver a rich snippet in the results, "what are rich snippets", "how to get started in real estate", "how to increase your blog traffic", and so on...

WHY YOU NEED TO FOCUS ON RICH RESULTS.

Considering banging your head against the wall, wondering why you're reading such a soul-destroying dry topic? Well, don't throw this book out the window just yet...

These new technologies allow greater control over search listings, making it easier for search engines to crawl your site, potentially featuring your content as a "rich result" appearing at the top of the results, helping you get higher click-through rates and get more eyeballs on content. Think of this technology like meta tags on steroids...

Still not convinced? With 40% of voice search results originating from rich results, targeting rich results is a must if you want to get amongst the rising voice search trend.

WHY USE STRUCTURED DATA AND JSON-LD?

To tell Google which parts of your content you want to be considered for a rich result, you need to use code called "structured data." With new technologies, as always, there's a debate about the best to use—JSON-LD, RDFa, microdata, the list goes on...

I won't waste your time with a technical debate. Google has openly stated JSON-LD is the preferred code—and made it clear not to mix structured data technologies for fear of confusing the search engine spider...

We're here for high rankings and traffic, not a lengthy diatribe on each individual technology, so let's go with what Google recommends for the purposes of this book— JSON-LD.

HOW TO GET STARTED WITH JSON-LD.

So, what does all this JSON-LD structured data stuff look like? Let's look at a business listing to see how it should be coded, according to Google's recommendations.

```
<script type="application/ld+json">
{
  "@context": "https://schema.org",
  "@type": "Organization",
  "url": "http://www.example.com",
  "name": "Unlimited Ball Bearings Corp.",
  "contactPoint": {
```

```
  "@type": "ContactPoint",
  "telephone": "+1-401-555-1212",
  "contactType": "Customer service"
  }
}
</script>
```

The JSON-LD example code from Google gives the search engine a friendly nudge to recognize the information as a business listing, such as the name and the phone number.

While the above example will be just enough if you have a simple business listing, you or your developer will have to use Google's documentation and tools, listed later in this chapter, to ensure your code is implemented correctly.

Different Types of Rich Results Supported by Google.

Google supports the below rich results. If you have any of these content types on your site, you can benefit from Google's recommended additional code.

- Article
- Book
- Breadcrumb
- Carousel
- Course
- Critic review
- Dataset
- Employer Aggregate Rating
- Event
- Fact Check
- FAQ

- How-to
- Job Posting
- Job Training (beta)
- Local Business Listing
- Logo
- Movie
- Occupation
- Product
- Q&A
- Recipe
- Review snippet
- Sitelinks Searchbox
- Software App (beta)
- Speakable (news content)
- Subscription and paywalled content
- Video

Holy cow! That's a lot of different search result types. Fortunately, Google has listed them neatly with example code on the following page.

Structured data markup that Google Search supports – Google
https://developers.google.com/search/docs/appearance/structured-data/search-gallery

You can also use the Merkle Schema Markup Generator to automatically generate the code for you. The Merkle Schema Markup Generator is a free tool that generates the code for you. All you have to do is select the type of rich snippet you are targeting (e.g. a local business, a recipe, a FAQ page), type in as much information as possible, and it will print out the recommended code, ready to paste directly into your website.

Schema Markup Generator - Merkle
https://technicalseo.com/tools/schema-markup-generator/

Finally, when you or your developer are testing the code on your site, use Google's Structured Data Testing Tool and make sure the code is implemented correctly. And use Google's Rich Results Test to preview how your page can appear in the search results.

Structured Data Testing Tool - Google
https://developers.google.com/search/docs/appearance/structured-data

Rich Results Test – Google
https://search.google.com/test/rich-results

HOW TO TARGET FEATURED SNIPPET RANKINGS IN GOOGLE'S SEARCH RESULTS.

After you've uploaded a bunch of fancy JSON-LD code to your site, you're probably wondering when you appear at the top of the results... Using JSON-LD is just one step, if you want to achieve the coveted featured snippet ranking, you'll need to satisfy the following requirements.

1. Rank on the first page, first. Almost all featured snippets are fetched from rankings on the first page. Follow techniques from the On-Page SEO and Link building chapter and work your way up the results first.

2. Create "snippet bait" targeting 40-50 words. SEMrush did a giant study on rich results and featured snippets, finding almost all text-based rich snippets range between 40 to 50 words.

3. Structure your content to target featured snippets. Hint: putting target keywords as H2 or H3 headings, followed by clear and concise paragraphs around 40-50 words, is a solid approach.

5. Use images. Featured snippets often contain images, I like to call them "snimmages"—for some reason, this terminology never really caught on like I hoped... Using images increases chances for both text and images appearing in the featured snippet. According to Google's official guidelines, images should be at least 1200 pixels wide. And using multiple high-resolution images with aspect ratios of 16x9, 4x3, and 1x1 can help with appearing on different devices.

HOW TO TARGET "PEOPLE ALSO ASK" AND QUESTION-BASED RICH RESULTS.

Google   what is the keto diet   🎤 🔍

🔍 All   ▶ Videos   🖼 Images   📰 News   🛒 Shopping   ⋮ More   Settings   Tools

About 159,000,000 results (0.63 seconds)

The Ketogenic Diet: A Detailed Beginner's Guide to Keto
https://www.healthline.com › nutrition › ketogenic-diet-101 ▾
Jul 30, 2018 - The ketogenic diet is a very low-carb, high-fat diet that shares many similarities with the Atkins and low-carb diets. It involves drastically reducing carbohydrate intake and replacing it with fat. This reduction in carbs puts your body into a metabolic state called ketosis. A Ketogenic Diet to Lose · I Tried the Keto Diet to Manage · Keto-Friendly Fast Food

People also ask

What can you eat on the keto diet?   ⌄

How do I start the keto diet?   ⌄

Is the keto diet Safe 2019?   ⌄

Why keto diet is bad?   ⌄

                                                        Feedback

There's another popular type of rich snippet appearing for almost any question type search—the "People also ask" rich snippet. Fortunately, some clever SEOs have figured out general techniques for targeting these sexy rankings.

1. Your desired ranking must be a question-type keyword. Searches not phrased as a question won't always trigger a "People always ask" snippet, so it's best to focus on question-type keywords.

2. Your answer should be clear and concise. Well-written and clear answers have a much greater chance of being featured than poorly written answers. Remember the 40-50 words technique from earlier in this chapter.

3. Include a Q&A or how-to section on your site. Increase content in a question-and-answer format and increase your odds of being featured for question-type searches.

4. Provide more valuable information than a simple and direct answer. If your answer has numbered lists, rich media such as images and videos, and is generally more helpful than an obvious answer to the question, then you have a greater chance of being featured.

5. Add Google's recommended question-type JSON-LD code to relevant pages... While this won't guarantee results, it'll encourage Google to look at your pages and consider them for use in the rich results. Recommended JSON-LD code is listed on each of the following pages.

FAQ Structured Data - Google Search
https://developers.google.com/search/docs/appearance
/structured-data/faqpage

How-to Structured Data - Google Search
https://developers.google.com/search/docs/appearance
/structured-data/how-to

Q&A – Structured Data, Google Search
https://developers.google.com/search/docs/appearance
/structured-data/qapage

6. Use the Also Asked tool to find questions people are searching for. The Also Asked tool tells you the "People Also Ask" questions that appear on any topic. You can use this information to improve your chances to appear for multiple results.

"People Also Ask" keyword research - Also Asked
https://alsoasked.com/

VOICE SEARCH SEO AND GOOGLE'S SPEAKABLE STRUCTURED DATA.

With the rise of the miniature circular voice-speaking robots invading people's homes—virtual assistants like Alexa and Google Assistant—it comes with little surprise Google is making moves to capture this market, and you can too!

Before we cover Google's "Speakable" markup, and how any business can optimize for voice search, you might be wondering why voice search is important—after all, you want customers to read content on your site, not have it spoken aloud, right?

Well, not necessarily... If voice searchers find a solid voice answer, they are likely to visit your site. Voice search is in an upward trend and best viewed as an additional source of traffic, not something that will take away from current traffic. Now we've established it's worthwhile putting voice search optimization on the radar, let's jump into the gritty details.

Implementing Speakable for US-based news publishers.

Implementing Speakable is straightforward. Firstly, you need to be a US-based news publisher. Secondly, you need to submit your site for consideration in Google's Publisher Center. Finally, you will need to direct your site developer to review Schema.org's technical guidelines and implement the code on your site. Review the following resources and get started.

Google - Speakable and Submission for Eligibility
https://developers.google.com/search/docs/appearance/structured-data/speakable#eligibility

Schema.org - Speakable Developer Documentation
https://schema.org/speakable

Voice Search Optimization for regular site owners and marketers.

We're not all US-based news publishers and it's understandable regular site owners and marketers want to jump on the voice search bandwagon. While voice search optimization is new, a handful of techniques have been established by industry insiders. Implement these and you will increase your chances of having your words of wisdom echoed by a voice-speaking robot in a stranger's home.

- Short answers in substantial content... Pages with over 2000 words appear more frequently in search results than articles with 500 or so words. Within long-form content, including short-form content, in a question and answer format, using short and concise answers, following the 40-50 word rule mentioned earlier.
- 65% of voice search results use HTTPS and have SSL certificates installed... If you've read this far and haven't installed an SSL certificate, I'm starting to get a little concerned.
- Focus on building an authoritative site in your niche— relevant links, high-value content, active social profiles, and so on.
- Make sure your website loads fast—4.6 seconds or faster to be precise. A large portion of voice searches are performed on mobile devices with slow Internet connections.

FACEBOOK OPEN GRAPH.

While we know schema.org is the best approach for adding metadata to your site, there is one additional metadata technology you should also use.

Facebook's Open Graph language allows you to determine how your site listing appears when shared on Facebook.

If you do not include Facebook's Open Graph code on your site, when a user shares your content on Facebook it will show a plain listing on the news feed, putting the responsibility on the user to describe the article and make it worth reading. But if you do include Facebook Open Graph code, it comes up looking sexy, just like your search listings if you have been using your meta title and meta description tags correctly.

By putting your best foot forward, and making your listing show up correctly on Facebook, you will encourage more customers to click on your site and increase the number of likes and shares for your page. This will increase the overall social signals of the page.

Here's an example of properly formatted meta code using Facebook Open Graph. As you can see, there are only minor tweaks required to make your page show up nicely on Facebook's news feed. So go ahead and use it on your site!

```
<title>Buy Baseball Jackets Online</title>
<meta property='og:type' content='site'>
```

```
<meta property-'og:description' name='description'
content='Wide range of Baseball Jackets online, for all
leagues and players. Free delivery and free returns both
ways in USA.'/>
```

If you're worried about confusing search engines by using
several "structured data" technologies at the same time,
such as Open Graph and schema.org, don't worry, you
won't have any problems.

Facebook Open Graph is mainly used by Facebook's web
crawler, not by search engines, so you can use Open
Graph and schema.org in tandem without any problems.

If you want to read up further on Facebook's Open Graph,
or if you have complex types of listings on your site, check
out Facebook's Open Graph guide below.

Open Graph Protocol
https://ogp.me/

10. POWERFUL SEO TOOLS.

The following tools can help find link-building opportunities, diagnose site issues, create easy-to-understand SEO reports, make Google crawl your site faster, and much more. Ultimately, the following tools make it easier to achieve high rankings, and can potentially save hours, days, or weeks of time.

Are there more SEO tools out there than in this list? Sure. SEO tools are a dime a dozen. The following is a selection of the tools I have found useful and to list out the tools mentioned in this book, for ease of reference. Some are free, some are paid, but most offer a free trial long enough to start optimizing your site. I have no affiliation with any of these sites, I've just listed tools that I find useful. So, jump in and have fun.

RESEARCH TOOLS.

Also Asked - Free and paid plans
https://alsoasked.com/

The Also Asked tool tells you the "People Also Ask" questions that appear on any topic. You can use this information to improve your chances to appear for multiple rich snippet search results.

KWfinder
https://kwfinder.com/

KWFinder is a fairly new research tool to the market, providing traffic data for keywords, estimated SEO difficulty, competitive data on sites ranking in the top 10, and much more. Its well-rounded feature set means you could use this tool alone for your keyword research without having to use multiple tools. Plans start at $49 per month.

Google Ads Keyword Planner
https://ads.google.com/home/tools/keyword-planner/

The Google Ads Keyword Planner has been mentioned several times throughout this book for good reason, it allows you to download estimated traffic for keywords users are typing into Google's search box—powerful knowledge to have in your SEO toolkit. You can see how many times a keyword has been searched in Google in granular detail. You can narrow this down by country and device type, including mobile phones and so on. During recent years, Google has clamped down on the free data available to non-paying users, to access all the research data you will need an active Google Ads campaign and must be regularly spending at least a modest amount of money.

Google Trends -Free
https://trends.google.com/trends/

Google Trends provides powerful stats on search trends over time. Great for seeing how your market performs overall, and how demand changes over time for your keywords.

Moz - Free and Paid.
https://moz.com/free-seo-tools

No book on SEO would ever be complete without a mention of Moz. Moz offers keyword analysis, brand monitoring, rankings tracking, on-page SEO suggestions, search engine crawl tests, and much more. This is an essential toolbox for every SEO practitioner, from beginner to advanced.

Ahrefs SEO Toolbar - Free
https://ahrefs.com/seo-toolbar

The Ahrefs SEO toolbar gives you a powerful set of stats for any site you visit, right within your browser.

A great tool for snooping on competitors and doing market research.

Ubersuggest - Free
https://neilpatel.com/ubersuggest/

Automatically download the auto-suggested keywords from Google's search results for a nice, juicy collection of long-tail keywords.

LSIGraph: LSI Keyword Generator
https://lsigraph.com/

Generate semantic, long-tail, and LSI keyword suggestions. Great for both SEO and PPC campaigns.

Answer The Public
https://answerthepublic.com/

Answer The Public crawls the web and generates a massive list of questions your customers are asking, across the Internet, related to your keyword.

OPTIMIZATION TOOLS.

Google Page Speed Insights - Free
https://pagespeed.web.dev/

Google Page Speed Insights is a fantastic tool provided by Google to help speed up your site. Google Page Speed Insights will give you a score on how well your load time is performing, and provide a simple set of suggestions to forward to your developers and speed up your site.

Google SERP Snippet Optimization Tool - Free
https://www.highervisibility.com/seo/tools/serp-snippet-optimizer/

This handy little tool lets you type out title tags and meta tags and see a live preview of how your site will appear in the search results.

Google Search Console - Free
https://search.google.com/search-console/welcome

Google Search Console is another great tool. If you haven't got Google Search Console set up, drop what you are doing and set it up now!

Google Search Console will report urgent messages if there are any severe problems when Google comes along and crawls your site. You can also submit your sitemap directly to Google from within Google Search Console, meaning you know Google has been given a friendly nudge to come around and pick up all the content on your site. This is a must-have SEO tool for every site.

HTTP Status Code Checker
https://httpstatus.io/

If you have ever set up a URL redirect or asked your developer to, it's always a good idea to check and ensure the redirect has been set up correctly.

Use the redirect checker to make sure your redirects are returning successful responses to the web browser, so you can feel confident Google is picking it up properly too.

Lighthouse – Chrome Developers
https://developer.chrome.com/docs/lighthouse/overvie
w/

Lighthouse provides reports on website performance, accessibility, adherence to programming best practices, SEO, and more—with actionable steps on improving each of these areas. Lighthouse is best suited for advanced developers working on complicated projects, as opposed to finding easily identifiable improvements for simple websites.

Robots.txt Analyzer - Free
http://tools.seobook.com/robots-txt/analyzer/

Many robots.txt files can often have slight errors that are difficult to pick up, especially for larger sites. Run your robots.txt file through this tool for a free analysis to see if there are any errors.

Robots.txt Generator -Free
https://nobsmarketplace.com/resources/tools/robots-txt-generator/

If you're lazy like I am, you'll love this free robots.txt generator. Works great for both basic and advanced robots.txt users to create robots.txt files quickly and easily.

Schema Markup Generator - Free
https://technicalseo.com/tools/schema-markup-generator/

Great and easy-to-use tool to automatically generate your rich snippets markup.

Screaming Frog SEO Spider - Free version available
https://www.screamingfrog.co.uk/seo-spider/

Screaming Frog SEO Spider is one of the most powerful SEO tools available, that will crawl your entire site, or a list of links, and offer very powerful and juicy stats. Such as stats on which pages have 404 errors, 301 redirects, server errors, title tags, meta desc tags, and the list goes on! This tool has been around for years and is a must-have tool for the advanced SEO practitioner.

XML Sitemaps - Free trial available
https://www.xml-sitemaps.com/

XML Sitemaps is a fantastic tool for creating an XML sitemap to submit to Google. Useful for sites that do not have a built-in XML sitemap functionality.

The tool automatically formats the sitemap so it is in the right format for Google and other search engines. With XML Sitemaps you can create a sitemap for your site within minutes.

LINK-BUILDING TOOLS.

Link Clump
https://github.com/benblack86/linkclump

Possibly one of my favorite tools. Link Clump is a free Chrome extension that allows you to highlight and copy all the links on the page in one click. Great for copying the Google search results into a spreadsheet, without having to individually visit each page.

Ahrefs - $99 per month.
https://www.ahrefs.com/

Ahrefs offers arguably the most up-to-date index of links pointing to websites and a highly accurate tool for analyzing links pointing to your site—and to your competitors. It also offers other competitive data, like keyword suggestions and estimated traffic numbers, so you can be sneaky and copy keyword ideas from your competitors.

Buzzstream - Free trial and paid plans.
https://www.buzzstream.com/

Buzzstream is the darling of many link builders and content marketers. It is an end-to-end outreach platform, meaning it can find contact details, send emails, track relationships, and more. Buzzstream doesn't allow automatic follow-ups nor one-click sending for your campaigns, so a bit of manual work is required to run campaigns through Buzzstream.

Hunter

https://hunter.io/

Hunter is purely focused on finding contact details and is very good at it. It has a nice Chrome plugin that shows you all the contact details it can find for a particular site while browsing. Free plans include up to 100 contact information requests.

Mailshake

https://mailshake.com

Mailshake is pure-outreach. You will need to provide contact information yourself. It is effective at sending personalized email campaigns, and you can import all the personalization info including name, address, and a personal message via CSV file. Includes automatic follow-ups, email template libraries, and more.

Ninja Outreach

https://ninjaoutreach.com/

Ninja Outreach is another end-to-end outreach platform, including finding contact details, sending emails, personalization, automatic follow-ups, and more. I have noticed the majority of bloggers on this platform ask for you to pay to contribute to their site, which is a downside in my opinion.

Pitchbox

https://pitchbox.com/

Pitchbox is an enterprise-level outreach platform, including finding contact details, personalized emails, automated follow-ups, detailed reporting, and more. Pitchbox is more suited for larger teams or campaigns, SEO agencies, and SEO professionals. It comes at a higher price point, but it is sometimes the preferred tool for serious SEO guys and gals, due to having more features and flexibility than the other platforms.

Moz - Link Explorer - Free for limited access and paid plans for pro users.
https://moz.com/link-explorer

Link Explorer is a must for understanding the links pointing to your site and competitors' sites. Cheeky little tricks with Link Explorer include exporting competitors' backlinks and looking over these links for opportunities to build links to your site. For a higher level of detail, I do prefer Ahrefs when it comes to analyzing links, but Moz's ease of use and simple design for beginners make it a solid choice for SEO newbies.

WEB ANALYTICS TOOLS.

Google Analytics
https://analytics.google.com/analytics/web/

Google Analytics is the market leader in web analytics, and the best part is it's free. It allows you to track the visitors on your site, where they came from, and how much money they spent if you are running an online store, and you can track online inquiries if you are running a local business. It's an essential tool for every website.

Call Rail
https://www.callrail.com/

Call Rail is popular for its ease of use, international support, integrations with Google Analytics, Google Ads, WordPress, and Salesforce, and flexibility. It also includes cool features like text messaging, geo-routing, voicemail, and more.

Call Tracking Metrics
https://www.calltrackingmetrics.com/

Call Tracking Metrics is another popular platform, also offering international support, Google Analytics, Google Ads, WordPress integrations, and overall, similar features to Call Rail. Some online user reports mention preferring Call Rail for its simplicity and flexibility and found Call Tracking Metrics a little difficult to navigate, but in the end, it's often best to trial both platforms initially and see what works best for your business. Plans start at $39 per month.

Crazy Egg - Free to start and paid professional plans.
https://www.crazyegg.com/

If you want a visual indication of how visitors behave on your site once they arrive, Crazy Egg is a fantastic tool. With Crazy Egg, you can get heat maps of where visitors click on the page. You can also see heat maps of how far visitors scroll down the page.

Looker Studio by Google
https://lookerstudio.google.com/overview

Google's Looker Studio will create visual reports so you can monitor almost anything—calls, ad campaigns on various platforms, search rankings, Salesforce leads, your bookkeeping system, and the list goes on. The best part is, it's free.

BONUS CHAPTER 1: GOOGLE'S ALGORITHM UPDATES.

You need to be informed about Google's updates to ensure your site doesn't trigger Google's spam filters. In some cases, you can take advantage of updates to the algorithm and get higher rankings. In this chapter, I will walk you through the biggest updates you should be aware of. And at the end of this chapter, I will show you resources for catching wind of new updates. Let's get started.

GOOGLE'S HELPFUL CONTENT UPDATE (A.K.A. GOOGLE'S SECRET NEW RANKING FACTOR).

Much to the chagrin of the SEO community, Google announced an impending A.I. update on August 2022, just a few weeks before it was expected to go live.

You know it's going to be big when Google pre-announces an update, which is why this update was expected to turn the industry upside down. SEO pros scrambled to check their search rankings weren't about to disappear into a black hole. Site owners threw their hands in the air wondering what to do. And SEO bloggers went into a heated frenzy, churning out articles and analyses around the clock, trying to predict the impact of this update.

And when the update was finally released, it was met with... crickets.

The "Helpful Content Update", was completed on September 9, 2022. And while the actual impact appeared to be small — so small some industry analysts actually got cheesed off — this is a much, much bigger update disguised as a small update. So, let's dive into the gritty details.

What is the Helpful Content Update?

According to the official word from Google HQ — brace yourself, we're about to get technical — Google's Helpful Content Update is a site-wide, weighted, continuous, artificial intelligence classifier search signal...

Simple words? Google now uses AI to detect if your content sucks.

It makes sense that Google does this when you think about it...

Instead of picking out one or two bad things spammy websites are doing each year and then kicking them out of the search results (what Google did in the past), Google uses this new AI system to automatically determine if your content sucks. Google then uses this information as a ranking factor to calculate the search results, so it's always running in the background.

So overall, websites showing up high in the search results have really good, helpful content. And websites with really spammy, unhelpful content appear lower in the search results.

But how do we know if our content sucks? Well, I'm glad you asked. Google released a series of guidelines to make sure our content doesn't get labeled as bad. Let's take a look at the official guidance from Google.

People-first content (a.k.a, good content).
- Do you have an existing or intended audience for your business or site that would find the content useful if they came directly to you?
- Does your content clearly demonstrate first-hand expertise and a depth of knowledge (for example, expertise that comes from having actually used a product or service, or visiting a place)?
- Does your site have a primary purpose or focus?
- After reading your content, will someone leave feeling they've learned enough about a topic to help achieve their goal?
- Will someone reading your content leave feeling like they've had a satisfying experience?
- Are you keeping in mind our guidance for core updates and for product reviews?

Search engine-first content (a.k.a., bad content).
- Is the content primarily to attract people from search engines, rather than made for humans?
- Are you producing lots of content on different topics in hopes that some of it might perform well in search results?

- Are you using extensive automation to produce content on many topics?
- Are you mainly summarizing what others have to say without adding much value?
- Are you writing about things simply because they seem trending and not because you'd write about them otherwise for your existing audience?
- Does your content leave readers feeling like they need to search again to get better information from other sources?
- Are you writing to a particular word count because you've heard or read that Google has a preferred word count?

What creators should know about Google's August 2022 helpful content update - Google Search Central
https://developers.google.com/search/blog/2022/08/hel pful-content-update

In other words, Google wants you to be making content that's original, helpful, and at least somehow related to the main topic of your website. If this sounds like you, then you're fine. You don't have anything to worry about.

If you're churning out mass-produced content that's been copied from other sites, you could be in trouble. If this sounds like you, it's a good idea to read Google's official documentation and get an outside opinion before making changes. And confirm you definitely had traffic problems when this update was released.

If you're confident you have "bad content", follow Google's official guidance to remove unhelpful and irrelevant content from your website, and you will naturally recover within a month or two. And if your site already has significant levels of traffic, only make changes if you're entirely confident you were negatively affected by this update.

GOOGLE'S SEPTEMBER 2022 CORE UPDATE.

On September 2022, Google had the gall to release a Core Update, right after the Helpful Content Update, and the Link Spam Update, making it almost impossible to figure out what was in this update. The gall!

Does that mean we should throw our clothes out of the window, drink a bottle of tequila, and wander the streets in a fugue state, only to be picked up by the police at 5 am? No. We put our detective hats on and use our powers of deduction to figure out what Google changed. It sounds crazy, but it works! So put that bottle of tequila away and let's look at what happened.

What was affected?

Google finished rolling out the update on September 12, 2022. As a rule, Google's core updates aren't focused on one or two small things and instead focus on how Google assesses a website's content overall.

That said, industry analysts made the following observations about this update...

- Industries the most affected include Online Communities, Hobbies & Leisure, Pets & Animals, Beauty & Fitness, and Games.

- Sites that lost traffic and search rankings had large amounts of copied or unoriginal content.

- Other negatively affected sites aggregated content from other well-known sites.

- And some negatively affected sites had trust and privacy issues (like asking for a user's emails on the homepage or not making ownership of the website clear).

What to do if affected by a Core Update.

Google is famously coy about their Core Updates—they don't want anyone to know the gritty details! But if you've been hit by one of these updates, there is a process you can follow to improve your site so when the next Core Update comes around you can see an increase in traffic.

The most important practice to follow with Core Updates is this—if it ain't broke, don't fix it. Don't go around changing things on websites with large levels of traffic, unless you are really confident you were affected by the update or you really know what you are doing.

If you think you've been affected by this update, the first thing to do is look at your traffic and figure out if you were actually affected by the update. Look at your traffic and search rankings around September 12, 2022. If you see a sharp decrease in traffic and search rankings on this date (i.e. it looks like it fell off a cliff) then you may need to fix up your site. And you'll need to review the following areas:

1. Content quality. Is your content unique, useful, and valuable for users? Or is your content thin, superficial, not original, artificial, and not really helpful?

2. Expertise & Authoritativeness. Are you qualified to be publishing on the topic? Or are you publishing on sensitive topics that can affect users' well-being, with no expertise or credentials?

3. Presentation and production. Are the content and design on your site produced sloppily? Is it difficult for users to get to the main content on your site?

4. Compare your website to competing sites. Does your content answer user's questions better than competitors or worse?

If negatively affected by a Core Update, it's a good idea to review Google's guidelines in full at the following page, and if your website has a large volume of traffic and search rankings consider getting expert help.

Google Search's core updates and your website
https://developers.google.com/search/updates/core-updates

GOOGLE'S OCTOBER 2022 SPAM UPDATE.

On October 2022, Google tried to slip one by us by quietly announcing a spam update on their search updates page. Fortunately for us, some super smart SEO professionals (who have nothing better to do) picked up the tiny change on Google's search updates page, put on their detective hats, and started digging around, looking for clues on what to do.

About once per year, Google improves its technology for picking up spam and then karate chops the dodgy sites out of the search results. This is an important time to pay attention if you're doing anything just slightly risky, like affiliate marketing and creating large amounts of low-quality content, or low-quality links.

Look over your traffic around October 21, 2022. If you had massive changes in traffic or rankings around this time, you might have been hit by Google's super smart artificial intelligence-powered spam detection robot called SpamBrain.

What is SpamBrain?

SpamBrain is an AI-powered tool Google built to automatically pick up spam and hacked pages and boot them out of the search results. Every several months, Google's SpamBrain looks at your website, and your content and decides one thing — are you a spammer? If you are, look out! Because your search rankings might just disappear off a cliff.

What to do about SpamBrain and spam updates?

If you're ever negatively affected by a spam update by Google, here's the good news. All you have to do is to remove the offending content or practices from your website completely, show Google that your site has improved over several months (it will be detected automatically), and you can recover. Look over the following list from Google's spam guidelines, see if anything looks familiar, and remove it from your site.

If none of the words on the list make sense to you, then you can take a deep breath. You're probably fine. It's almost impossible to be doing these things by mistake, so you have to have to be doing this stuff on purpose before getting in trouble for it.

Things in Google's spam policy you shouldn't be doing...

- Cloaking.
- Doorways.
- Hacked content.
- Hidden text and links.

- Keyword stuffing.
- Link spam.
- Machine-generated traffic.
- Malware and malicious behaviors.
- Misleading functionality.
- Scraped content.
- Sneaky redirects.
- Spammy automatically-generated content.
- Thin affiliate pages.
- User-generated spam.

Google Search Spam Updates and Your Site - Google Search Central
https://developers.google.com/search/updates/spam-updates

Spam Policies for Google Web Search - Google Search Central
https://developers.google.com/search/docs/essentials/spam-policies

GOOGLE'S FEBRUARY 2023 PRODUCT REVIEWS UPDATE.

Google has done it again—another update to its product reviews system, leaving affiliate SEOs scrambling to make sense of the changes. Fear not, SEO aficionados, because we'll break down the February 2023 Product Reviews Update, shed some light on what happened, and cover action steps if affected.

What happened?

On February 2023, Google released its Product Reviews Update, focused on rewarding high-quality product reviews that provide insightful analysis, original research and are written by experts or enthusiasts who truly know their stuff.

This update was completed on March 7th and released in multiple languages, including English, Spanish, German, French, Italian, Vietnamese, Indonesian, Russian, Dutch, Portuguese, and Polish. The number of languages it's released in indicates that it's a global update, which means that it's a big one.

If you're an e-commerce site owner, blogger, or publisher with a large number of product reviews, you'll want to pay close attention to this update. The changes primarily evaluate product reviews on a page-level basis, but if a significant portion of your site is dedicated to product reviews, your entire site could be affected.

Since the update, Google now prioritizes product reviews that demonstrate firsthand knowledge and expertise of the products and is now paying extra attention to in-depth research, original analysis, and expert opinions in product reviews.

Action steps if affected.

If you think the update has affected your site, it's important to look over your traffic and rankings around February 2023. If your traffic is stable, then you probably shouldn't change anything. But if your traffic fell off a cliff on February 2023, you may need to improve the quality of your product reviews by:

1. Evaluating products from a user's perspective.
2. Demonstrating your expertise and knowledge of the products.
3. Provide evidence of your experiences with the product, such as photos or videos.
4. Sharing quantitative measurements of the product's performance.
5. Comparing the product with competitors and discussing different use cases.
6. Identifying key decision-making factors and how the product performs in those areas.

Remember, content that was impacted by a product reviews update might not recover until the next update. However, Google's assessment of product review content is just one of many ranking factors, so changes can happen at any time for various reasons.

Best practices for product reviews.

Overall, if you've been affected or not, it's generally best to follow Google's best practices to lessen your chances of being negatively affected by future updates.

To ensure your product reviews continue to thrive in the search results, follow these best practices:

1. Describe how a product has evolved from previous models/releases.
2. Explain the product's design choices and their impact on users.
3. Include links to other useful resources and multiple sellers.
4. When recommending a product, provide firsthand supporting evidence, such as photos or videos.
5. Demonstrate expertise in the subject matter.

You can check out Google's official guidelines on product reviews on the following page...

Write high-quality product reviews - Google Search Central
https://developers.google.com/search/docs/specialty/ecommerce/write-high-quality-product-reviews

GOOGLE'S BARD VERSUS CHAT GPT - THE VICIOUS BATTLE OF THE AI CHATBOTS.

In the rapidly changing digital landscape, we're witnessing a groundbreaking shift in how we interact with technology. While virtual assistants like Alexa and Siri have been around for some time, AI chatbots like ChatGPT and Google's Bard are taking the game to a whole new level, offering a 10x or even 100x improvement in their ability to respond to our questions.

These revolutionary tools use machine learning to mimic human conversation, transform how we access information, and create content with unparalleled precision and ease.

For the average person, this means having a virtual sidekick that's far more sophisticated and efficient than its predecessors, ready to help with anything from answering questions to writing code, making our digital lives more powerful than ever.

And right in front of our very eyes, a battle is unfolding between two AI chatbots. In one corner, we have Google's BARD, a newcomer to the ring. In the other, the heavyweight champion, ChatGPT. This face-off between the two AI titans is nothing short of fascinating. Let's take a closer look.

OpenAI's ChatGPT: the champion.

Launched in November 2022 by Elon Musk-funded AI lab OpenAI, ChatGPT became an overnight sensation, sparking widespread enthusiasm for AI products across the web. ChatGPT users found they could have natural conversations, write songs, essays, blog posts—and even write code—in just a few seconds with ChatGPT's powerful technology.

GPT-4, released in March 2023, continues to build on its success with more accurate results. Now backed by Microsoft, ChatGPT has even found its way into the Bing search engine, hinting at how the technology could disrupt Google's long-standing search market dominance.

Google's Bard: the challenger.

Introduced by Sundar Pichai, Google's CEO, in February 2023, BARD faced initial internal criticism for its rushed development in response to ChatGPT. Regardless, Google released BARD in March 2023, inviting users in the USA and UK to join a waitlist. Built on Google's LaMDA technology, BARD aims to be a "launchpad for creativity," despite occasional inaccuracies, as seen during a live demo involving the James Webb Space Telescope.

Google's BARD, like ChatGPT, gives users a chat interface to brainstorm ideas, recipes, blog posts, ideas for parties, or email responses, and if the user wants more information they can click through to the search results.

Google is almost a year behind its rival OpenAI in the development of this technology, which is innovating rapidly, so it's going to be interesting to see how this saga unfolds.

While both BARD and ChatGPT have their strengths and weaknesses, they provide unique opportunities for marketers, SEO professionals, and business owners. With the ability to blaze through certain tasks three or four times faster, those who adopt this technology quickly will have a major advantage over competitors who lag behind.

Practical insights for marketers and SEO professionals.

There are a few action steps you can take right now to stay ahead of this trend.

1. Embrace the AI-driven content creation wave. As AI chatbots like ChatGPT and BARD become more sophisticated, they'll increasingly be used for content creation, from writing blog posts and landing pages to drafting emails. Embrace these tools to streamline your content creation and stay ahead of the curve. This isn't something that you save for a rainy day.

2. Engage with AI chatbots as a user. Try chatbots like BARD and ChatGPT to familiarize yourself with their capabilities and limitations. By understanding how these tools work from a user's perspective, you'll be better equipped to direct your team to use them effectively in your marketing.

3. Understand the limitations of AI. While chatbots are evolving rapidly, they still have limitations, such as outdated knowledge or incorrect information. As a marketer, be mindful of these shortcomings. For example, you want to ensure that any AI-generated content is fact-checked and revised before it's published.

4. Monitor the space. It can't hurt to mosey on over to Bing once in a while and to keep an eye on AI chat competitors like You.com and Perplexity AI, as well as stay on top of any news, to stay informed about new technologies and strategies that could impact your marketing.

The rapid evolution of AI chatbots has a growing impact on the world of marketing. By adapting to these advancements, you can continue to thrive in a likely AI-dominated future.

GOOGLE'S MARCH 2023 CORE UPDATE: THE GOOD, THE BAD, AND THE UGLY.

Google has done it again, folks! The search engine giant unleashed the March 2023 Core Update, stirring up the digital marketing world like a tornado ripping through the SEO landscape. Grab your popcorn and sharpen your pencils, because we're about to take a deep dive into the chaos and look at what you need to know.

Official announcements by Google.

The first core update of 2023 began on March 15th, and Google estimates that the rollout may take up to two weeks to complete. As with all core updates, Google emphasizes that its primary focus is on improving how its systems assess content. So, if your site is affected, don't take it personally—Google is just trying to make the web a better place.

Analyzing the losers.

Now, let's talk about the websites that took a hit from this update. I've analyzed the top 20 negatively affected websites, as ranked by Sistrix, and found that they all committed a combination of the following SEO faux pas:

- Disastrous design.
- Content that's more ads than substance (40%-50% of content obscured).

- Desktop browsing experience marred by ads and popups (50% of content obscured).
- Mobile browsing experience reduced to a game of "Where's Waldo?" (90% of content obscured).
- Text so small you'd need a magnifying glass.
- Design straight out of the '90s (not in a cool, retro way).
- Site code with no actual content, and relying on iframes or JavaScript to populate the HTML.
- Homepages that offer no content about what the website is actually about (Wiktionary and Wikivoyage as examples).
- Sites hosting pirated or illegal content.
- Mobile designs that crumble like a cookie (not the tracking kind).

Best practices and action steps.

If you think your website has been affected by the March 2023 Core Update, don't panic! Instead, take a deep breath and follow these best practices and action steps:

- Review your site traffic on or around March 15th, 2023, and look for any steep changes. If you didn't experience any dropoffs, then it's probably best that you don't do anything.
- Review Google's advice on core updates and assess your content against their guidelines.
- Conduct a thorough audit of your site, focusing on pages that were negatively impacted and your homepage.
- Get an honest assessment of your site's content and design.
- Improve your mobile support.
- Take it easy on the ads.

- Take it easy on the popups.

Remember, core updates are a natural part of the evolution of the web, so it's best to look at them as an opportunity to learn, grow, and improve your site. If you've been staying on top of things, it's unlikely that you would have been affected.

Google Search's core updates and your website - Google Search Central
https://developers.google.com/search/updates/core-updates

GOOGLE'S COOKIELESS TRACKING UPDATE.

When you visit a website, it usually saves a little file on your computer called a cookie. Well, in a move to improve privacy across the web, in July 2023, Google Analytics will completely stop working for websites that haven't updated their code. And in late-2024, Google is going to completely phase out the use of cookies in the Google Chrome browser.

These changes will likely have a positive impact on improving our privacy across the Internet, which is very good.

But here's the thing, if you rely on web analytics right now, you rely on cookies to know how your website and ad campaigns are performing. So, when Google starts to phase out cookies, you could use lose important information to make your marketing campaigns run well.

It's a good idea to get ahead of this change and ensure the long-term success of your marketing campaigns. Here's a quick rundown.

What you need to know.

- In mid 2022, Google announced the slow phase-out of external cookies in the Google Chrome browser, giving business owners, advertisers, and publishers notice to update the tracking codes on their websites.
- On July 1, 2023, old Google Analytics accounts will stop processing data, so if you haven't already, you need to install Google Analytics 4 as soon as possible.
- In late 2024, the use of these files in web analytics and advertising campaigns will be completely disabled in the Google Chrome browser.
- If you don't update the tracking codes for your analytics and advertising campaigns on your website, you will eventually lose performance and conversion data — and we don't want that!

How to prepare for cookieless web analytics.

There are some simple steps to prepare for this update. If you're a non-technical person, no worries, simply discuss this list with your developer and skip to the next section. This process is best managed by a technical person, such as a web developer or marketer with a technical background.

1. Make sure you're using campaign URLs to track the performance of all of your online advertising campaigns.

2. Create a new Google Analytics 4 profile and install the tracking code on your website.

3. Enable Google Signals in Google Analytics 4, if you want information about conversions without the use of cookies.

4. If you have other analytics or ad campaigns running right now such as Meta Ads, you might want to start "scaling in" the new cookieless tracking codes, while leaving old tracking codes running, so you can make sure everything is running smoothly over several months.

5. Review the data in your analytics ad campaigns.

6. Set a date around mid-2024 to remove all of your old cookie-enabled tracking codes.

7. Be mindful of your load speed. Tracking codes have a tendency to really slow down your load times!

Campaign URL builder - Google
https://ga-dev-tools.web.app/ga4/campaign-url-builder/

Meet the next generation of Google Analytics – Google Analytics
https://support.google.com/analytics/answer/10089681

Google Analytics
https://analytics.google.com

KEEPING UP-TO-DATE WITH GOOGLE'S UPDATES.

As of the last couple of years, Google updates have become more frequent. While I understand the constant changes by Google might make you feel like throwing your hands in the air and doing a nudie run through the office, don't be disheartened. The following resources are great for staying updated. If there's a significant update to Google's algorithm, it will be covered on at least one of the following pages.

Google Algorithm Change History
https://moz.com/google-algorithm-change

Google PageRank & Algorithm Updates
https://www.seroundtable.com/category/google-updates

Google Search Central Blog
https://developers.google.com/search/blog

List of Google Search Ranking Updates - Google Search Central
https://developers.google.com/search/updates/ranking

GOOGLE'S 2023 UPDATES—WHAT'S ON THE HORIZON?

You don't need a crystal ball or secret informer at Google to get a sense of what's on the horizon. After reviewing decades of updates made to Google's search algorithm, or just previous months, it's easy to get an idea of what changes Google is likely to make.

Before looking at what's coming up, let's look at what previous Google updates have in common. Almost all previous updates can give us insights into upcoming updates. Previous updates generally focus on two things; 1) filtering out spam and low-quality websites, and 2) making the Internet and Google a better user experience.

To figure out what Google may be working on, we should look at possible improvements with these qualities, and updates Google has publicly acknowledged as being on the agenda.

1. Google makes improvements to search.

Google is constantly upgrading its most important product, search, so it safeguards its status as the most relevant search engine. Improvements include better technology to filter out spammy pages, better technology to understand difficult questions, and improvements to the search results. Google also releases Core Updates every 3-4 months, and this isn't expected to change anytime soon.

2. Google continues working on AI updates and AI chatbots evolve at the speed of light.

Artificial intelligence has been at the heart of Google's major changes in the past few years. AI has helped Google understand searches almost better than a human, detect spammy websites automatically, and personalize the search results based on how users behave. All of these changes indicate an overall trend, Google using AI to improve search results and strengthen its competitive advantage.

And recent breakthroughs in generative AI with chatbots like ChatGPT and Google's BARD are rapidly changing the way we work online. If you work in marketing, it pays to keep an eye on the overall AI trend.

3. Privacy improvements.

After years of privacy controversies plaguing tech companies, governments over the world are starting to wise up and are introducing new laws to protect how our personal data is handled by these companies. And Google is working to get ahead of this trend. Upcoming changes include Google Chrome's phase-out of cookies in 2024, privacy changes on Google's mobile devices, and the ability for users to request personal information to be removed from the search results. This overall trend is a win for user privacy, but will potentially reduce the effectiveness of online advertising.

4. Google and big tech capitalizes on everyone staying at home so much.

There's a weird trend happening in the world right now, the world is becoming a civilization of introverts and hermits who like to live and work at home. Whether you like it or not, the trend is real, and Google is working to be a part of this trend, with improvements to online shopping and how users interact with local businesses.

That covers probable areas of focus for Google over the next 12 months, based on current trends and what industry insiders believe we should focus on.

I am not a psychic and I can't see into the future. The above are just educated guesses. Don't run out and change your whole business based on speculation. That said, keep these areas in the back of your mind so you don't get caught with your pants down by a Google update.

Focus on improving quality and trust on your site, provide good mobile support, earn relevant backlinks, and improve user behavior on your site. If you focus on these areas it's unlikely you will run into major problems and you will increase your performance at the same time.

BONUS CHAPTER 2: THE QUICK AND DIRTY GUIDE TO PAY-PER-CLICK ADVERTISING WITH GOOGLE ADS.

WHY BOTHER WITH PAY-PER-CLICK ADVERTISING?

You would have to be as crazy as a box of weasels to pay each time someone visits your site with pay-per-click advertising, when you can rank high in Google for free, right?

Not necessarily. Pay-per-click advertising has some advantages over SEO, with PPC campaigns you can:

- Send customers to your site within hours, not the months it sometimes takes for solid SEO results.
- Track results down to the penny, and get very clear insights into the financial performance of your advertising. Simply set up conversion tracking with the instructions provided by Google, or whichever pay-per-click provider you choose.
- Achieve a much larger overall number of customers to your site by running pay-per-click in tandem with your other marketing efforts.
- In most cases, achieve a positive financial return on your marketing spend and keep on selling to these customers in the future.

There is one caveat to the last point. If you are a small fish trying to enter an extremely competitive market, such as house loans, insurance or international plane flights, it's likely the big players in the market are buying a large amount of advertising, forcing the average cost-per-click to astronomical prices, and making it difficult for new players to get a profitable return.

If you're selling pizza delivery in New York, pool cleaning in Los Angeles, or cheap baseball jackets... In other words, if you're selling a common local trade, service, or product online, it's likely you can receive a profitable return on your advertising spend.

While pay-per-click marketing really deserves its own book, this is a quick and dirty bonus chapter, jam-packed with just enough information to get a pay-per-click campaign set up, avoid common mistakes, and send more customers and sales to your business.

If you want to delve deeper into the science of pay-per-click advertising, I've included some great resources on Google Ads at the end of the chapter. Sound good? Let's get started.

WHICH IS THE BEST PPC PROVIDER TO START WITH?

There are many pay-per-click providers out there, Google Ads and Bing Ads are just two.

Google Ads text ads is generally the best starting point. You can sell anything on Google Ads if you have money to spend because the user base is so large.

If you're looking to jump into pay-per-click advertising, get started with Google Ads. Move on to the other pay-per-click networks after you have some experience under your belt.

Here's why I think Google Ads text ads are usually the best choice for a first venture into pay-per-click advertising:

- With Google's search engine market share at 88.61%, and Bing at 2.72%, you can reach out to the largest potential amount of customers with Google.
- Fast and instant results. Send new customers to your site within a couple of hours.
- Advanced targeting technology. Target users based on where they are located, or what browser or device they are using. Google's ad targeting technology is among the best in the world.
- Due to the popularity of Google Ads, there's a wealth of knowledge on running Google Ads campaigns successfully.

ENSURING SUCCESS WITH RESEARCH AND A PLAN.

Like all marketing projects, for a Google Ads campaign to be successful, you need to start with research and a solid plan. Without first defining your goals, and designing a robust strategy to achieve them, it's impossible to create a successful marketing campaign—you'll have no way of determining if the outcome is successful!

Here are some important questions to ask yourself before you get started:

- What is the objective of the campaign? Sales, web inquiries, sign-ups, or branding?
- What is the maximum monthly budget you can afford?
- What is the maximum cost-per-inquiry, or cost-per-sale you can afford? For example, if you are selling snow jackets at $100, and your profit margin is 20%, you really can't afford to spend much more than $20 on each customer you acquire. Write this figure down and review it later. You may need to first run a small test campaign to determine if pay-per-click is profitable, and the right tool for marketing your business.
- What are the most common characteristics of your customers? For example, if you're selling late-night pizza delivery in New York, you don't want to be paying for the lovely folk in Idaho searching for late-night pizza delivery. Write down your customers' common characteristics, and later in the settings recommendations, if there's an option to target these customers, I'll tell you how to target them.

HOW TO CHOOSE THE RIGHT KIND OF KEYWORDS.

It's the moment you've been waiting for. The keywords! Precious keywords.

Just like SEO, getting your keywords right with text ads is critical if you want a successful campaign.

Unlike SEO, with Google's text ads there are different types of keywords called keyword match-types. I've listed the main keyword match types below.

Broad match keywords.

The default type of keywords all Google Ads campaign use—if you don't change any settings—are broad match keywords. With broad match keywords, Google will take any word out of your phrase, and serve up ads for searches hardly related to your phrase.

Needless to say, almost all new campaigns should NOT be using broad match keywords to start with. Have a look at the example below.

keyword:
tennis shoes

will trigger ads for:
tennis
designer shoes
dress shoes
basketball shoes

tennis bags
tennis equipment

Phrase match keywords.

Phrase match keywords will only show your ad for searches containing your core phrase or close variations. With phrase match keywords, you can reach more customers while having a higher level of control over the relevancy of the traffic you're buying. And higher relevancy usually means more sales.

To enter a phrase match keyword, when adding keywords to your account, wrap the keywords with "" double quotation marks and these keywords will become phrase match keywords.

keyword:
"tennis shoes"

will trigger ads for:
tennis shoes
tennis shoes online
best tennis shoes
best shoe for tennis
where to buy shoes for tennis

will not match for:
tennis players
tennis rackets
margaret thatcher

Exact match keywords.

Exact match keywords will only trigger ads for the exact phrase you enter, and close variants. Needless to say, with exact match keywords in your campaign, you can have a high level of accuracy, and achieve more sales. Exact match keywords are indispensable for every Google Ads campaign.

To enter exact match keywords, wrap the keywords with [] square brackets when adding keywords to your account and they will become exact match keywords.

keyword:
[tennis shoes]

will trigger ads for:
tennis shoes
tennis shoe

will not match for:
mens tennis shoes
womens tennis shoes

Negative keywords.

One of the most important, but easily overlooked keywords are negative keywords. Negative keywords will prevent your ads from showing for searches that include your negative keyword.

If you are using phrase match or any kind of broad match keyword, you should be using negative keywords. Negative keywords are vital for ensuring you are not paying for advertising for irrelevant searches.

Enter negative keywords in your campaign by adding a - minus sign in front of your keywords when adding keywords, or going to the shared library on the left hand column in your Google Ads account, and you can apply negative keywords across your entire account, a great time-saving tip.

keywords:
car service
-guide
-manual

will trigger ads for:
car service los angeles
car service mechanic
car service tips

will not trigger ads for:
free car service guide
ford mustang 65 car service manual

When choosing keywords, you need a balance between keywords with a high level of accuracy, such as exact match keywords, and keywords with a larger amount of reach, such as phrase match.

Use a mix of the above keywords in your campaign, then review the performance of different keyword types after your campaign has been running, when you have some data.

STRUCTURING YOUR CAMPAIGN WITH AD GROUPS.

Google Ads offers an excellent way of organizing keywords called ad groups.

If you organize your campaign correctly with ad groups, you can quickly see which areas of your campaign are profitable and not so profitable.

Let's say you have a Harley Davidson dealership, with a wide range of HD gear from bikes to accessories and clothing, below is an example of ad groups you might create.

- Harley Davidson motorbikes
- Harley Davidson parts
- Harley Davidson accessories
- Harley Davidson jackets

With ad groups you can:

- Create multiple, and separate ads for each product line. Great for testing.
- Have a select range of keywords, specific to the ad group.
- Set a specific bid for the ad group. Great if you have higher-priced products or services you're willing to pay more for.

- Get detailed data on the performance of your ad groups and different products.

Structure your campaign with ad groups with a very clear and simple sense of organization when you set up your campaign. You'll get clearer performance insights, and it will make your life easier when you want to make improvements later on down the track.

HOW TO CRUSH THE COMPETITION WITH KILLER TEXT ADS.

Writing a killer text ad is essential to the success of your campaign. Poorly written ads can increase the overall costs of your campaign, sending less traffic to your site for more money. We don't want that.

With your text ads, you want to:

- Attract clicks from interested customers, not tire-kickers.
- Include keywords related to what the user searched for.
- Encourage a clear call to action and benefit for the user.

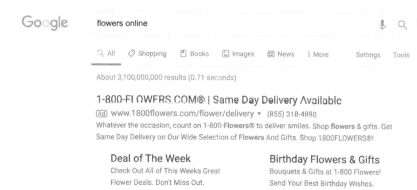

Text ads are made up of the following components:

1. Headline. Your headlines have a maximum of 30 characters. With your headline, you should include the keyword the user is searching for or capture the user's curiosity.

2. Description lines. You have two description lines at a maximum of 90 characters each. Your description lines should make it crystal clear what you are selling, the benefits of clicking through to your site and a call-to-action.

3. Display URL. You have 30 characters for a custom URL that will be displayed to users in the search results. Display URLs are great as you can actually display a different URL to the users than the URL of the page they will arrive on. You can take advantage of this to encourage more users to arrive on your site.

I've listed some winning ads so we can see why they are so successful:

In each of the above, we can see some similarities. Each ad has:

- An interesting headline. Each ad captures the curiosity of the user, through use of special characters, asking a question or posting a competitive offer right in the headline.
- Clear benefits. Each ad has a compelling offer in addition to the core product or service being sold, making the ad stand out from the search results, such as a no-risk, money-back guarantee, same-day delivery, or a free evaluation.
- A clear call-to-action. The first two ads make it clear what the next step should be. In the third ad, the call-to-action is not explicit, but it is obvious. By having "Online - $19.99" in the headline, and "Delivered Today", it is clear the user can order flowers online to be delivered the same-day.

HOW MUCH TO PAY FOR KEYWORDS.

A burning question for text ads newbies is, how much should I bid on my keywords?

There is no clear answer for finding your ideal bid price. You should only pay for what you can afford. You can find out how much you can afford by doing some simple math.

For example, let's look at an example scenario:

- You're selling video courses for $200.
- For every 100 visitors, 3 turn into customers. This is a conversion rate of 3%.
- If you bought 100 visitors at a cost-per-click of $3, this would cost $300.
- With your 3% conversion rate, you will have made $600 in sales, spent $300 on advertising, and made a profit of $300.

So, to calculate your ideal CPC, I'm sorry to say, you do need to sit down and do some math and figure it out. It can't be avoided. But to keep it simple, you should only pay what you can afford—otherwise you should be spending your marketing dollars elsewhere.

Here's the catch, you can only find out what your cost-per-click is after running your campaign for a while, when you have accumulated some data. So, run a small test campaign to begin with, to collect data. Use the information to make projections, and only pay what you can afford in a larger, more serious campaign.

In case you're wondering how prices get calculated, the Google Ads cost-per-click network uses a bidding system, which means you are taking place in an auction with competing advertisers. By increasing bids, your ad position increases, leading to more traffic or customers to your site.

Here is where it gets interesting. Google awards an advantage to advertisers showing ads with high quality and high relevancy. This is Google's Quality Score technology. Ads with a higher number of clicks and relevancy are awarded with a higher Quality Score, and subsequently receive increased ad positions and cheaper prices!

Keep this in mind when writing ads and choosing your keywords. Your ads should be relevant to achieve the highest Quality Score possible, so you can receive the cheapest cost-per-click.

GOOGLE ADS SETTINGS FOR GETTING STARTED.

The single most important factor to ensure your campaign is successful is to fill out all of the settings when you set up your campaign. Whatever you do, don't rush through the campaign settings, otherwise you will end up paying for advertising to people who have no interest in what you're selling.

I've listed recommended Google Ads settings below for reference, but if you are not setting up your Google Ads campaign right now, feel free to skip to the end of this chapter for closing recommendations on managing Google Ads campaigns for long-term success.

1. If you haven't done so already, create an account at https://ads.google.com/home/. When signing up, enter your Google account, or let the tool create one for you if you don't already have one.

2. Once fully signed in, click on the big button "Create your first campaign."

3. Campaign name:
Enter a descriptive name for your campaign.

4. Type:
Choose "search network only" from the drop-down. This is important. Make sure you select this option, unless you know what you are doing, otherwise you will also end up buying advertising on less relevant sites.

Select "All features - All options for the Search Network, with Display Select." Why would we want to restrict ourselves and give ourselves less options and features? Choose it, features are awesome. Trust me.

5. Networks:
Unselect "include search partners." We want to advertise on Google, not other smaller, potentially less-relevant sites.

6. Locations:
If you are targeting customers from a specific area, country, state or city, enter the most relevant setting for your customers here. Whatever you do, don't forget about this setting, otherwise if you're a local business you'll end up buying advertising halfway around the world!

7. Bid strategy:
Choose "I'll manually set my bids for clicks." This allows you to make sure you are only setting cost-per-click bids you can afford. More on setting bids later.

8. Default bid:
Enter any number here, we are going to change it later.

9. Budget:
Enter your daily budget.

10. Ad Extensions:
Ad Extensions, otherwise known as sitelinks, are a great way to encourage more clicks to your site. Enter as many relevant entries as you can, if you have an office address and phone number, use it.

11.   Schedule:
If you are only open during certain business hours, enter the hours you want to be running ads here. For some businesses, it's OK to run your campaign 24/7, because some customers will send an online inquiry if they arrive at your site outside of business hours. If you are selling something like a local food, such as a pizza shop, you might want to restrict your campaigns to only run during your opening hours.

12. Ad delivery:
Choose "Rotate indefinitely. Show lower performing ads more evenly with higher performing ads, and do not optimize."

Why would you want to choose this, you might wonder? You want to run your ads evenly, so you have reliable data when you review your ads, and can objectively see which ads are performing better for your goals.

You can leave the rest of settings for now, hit "save and continue", and you're good to go with setting up the rest of your campaign.

OPTIMIZATION TIPS FOR TWEAKING YOUR CAMPAIGN FOR BETTER PROFIT.

I've touched on a handful of secrets of starting successful pay-per-click campaigns, but now I'm going to cover the most important technique for ongoing pay-per-click success.

Review and improve your campaign regularly.

Leaving a Google Ads campaign running without keeping your head around the performance is like leaving a freight train running without a driver.

Regularly review your ad, ad group, keyword, cost-per-click, and cost-per-conversion performance. This will allow you to back the winning horses of your campaign and swiftly cut the losers.

Fortunately, the Google Ads platform offers endless opportunities for deep insights into the performance of your campaign.

As a starting point, below are example areas in your campaign to regularly look over:

- Ad group performance. Review click-through-rates, cost-per-click, and cost-per-conversion. Allocate more funds from your campaign to winning ad groups, and decrease funds or pause losing ad groups if you see any obvious trends.
- Ad performance. Look for winning ads with higher click-through-rates, lower cost-per-clicks, and lower cost-per-conversion. Pause expensive ads, and create new ads to split-test based on your winners. Progressively build up new ads with higher click-through-rates into your campaign over time.

- Keyword performance. Review which keywords are running at a higher cost, which keywords have low quality scores, and see if you can pause any overly budget-draining keywords with low conversions.

USING ACCELERATED MOBILE PAGES IN GOOGLE ADS CAMPAIGNS TO ACCELERATE YOUR SALES.

AMP significantly increases load speed for mobile users. Why is this important? Faster load times lead to higher conversion rates, and higher conversion rates lead to more sales. In fact, the smart lads over at Google's AMP team reported increases up to 80% in mobile conversion rates, and a 31% drop in bounce rates, in tests with a select few ecommerce retailers. If you're running a medium-to-large sized Google Ads campaign, it's worth taking a look.

To say implementing AMP is extremely technically involved would be an understatement — it's something that should only be handled by the deft hands of a highly skilled web developer, and beyond the scope of this book.

But the potential upside in sales make it worth a look for medium-to-large campaigns. You can forward the official documentation by Google below to your web developer to see if it can be done.

How to Use AMP With Google Ads - Google Ads
https://support.google.com/google-ads/answer/7495018

FURTHER GOOGLE ADS RESOURCES.

If you want to delve deeper into the pay-per-click rabbit hole, the resources below are a great starting point for anyone starting with pay-per-click advertising:

Ultimate Guide to Google AdWords - Perry Marshall

The *Ultimate Guide to Google Adwords* by Perry Marshall is often the starting point for many professionals starting out with PPC. Offers a great overview of Google Ads and delves into the inner game of successful Googel Ads campaigns. Great for beginners, but for more advanced techniques check out the following resources.

Advanced Google AdWords - Brad Geddes

If you want to be a pay-per-click guru, then look no further than this fantastic guide to advanced Google Ads management, great for both agencies and business owners running their own campaigns. Brad Geddes' magnum opus on advanced Google Ads pay-per-click advertising has been the secret treasure of many successful pay-per-click consultants, and readily available in Amazon and many other bookstores.

PPC Hero
https://www.ppchero.com/

PPC Hero is loaded with free advice on the latest Google Ads tricks and tips, but also covering fundamental pay-per-click methods that never change. Updated regularly.

Google Ads & Commerce Blog
https://blog.google/products/ads-commerce/

Google's official blog for Google Ads. Great for the latest Google Ads news direct from the horse's mouth.

That brings us to the end of the last bonus chapter of SEO 2023, and almost to the end of the book. Make sure you download the SEO checklist available on the following page as well as read through the final chapter for some final tips in ensuring your overall success in ranking high in the search results.

BONUS: COMPLIMENTARY 50-POINT SEO CHECKLIST PDF INSTRUCTIONS.

As a small thank you for reading this book, I've created a checklist summarising all of the major points for optimizing a website, and uploaded it to my website where it is regularly updated. It's in PDF because it's the format that is the most flexible for all readers and listeners — audiobook, paperback and ebook.

And I've created a free series of video tutorials. You can get them both at the following page.

Privacy minded folk, who don't want to join my free newsletter for readers can just click on 'no thanks, take me directly to the PDF' at the following webpage.

Complimentary SEO checklist and free videos – updated April 2023
https://www.simpleeffectiveness.com/seo-checklist

Get free tutorial videos, link building techniques and more in my exclusive newsletter for readers...

I often get emails from readers asking how to stay in touch, find out when I release new content and if I have other technical guides coming up in simple language, so I put together a newsletter. If you want to get...

- Step-by-step tutorial videos on SEO.
- New link building techniques.
- Find out about my latest books.
- A heads-up on super important changes to Google.
- Some extra (secret) updates for readers....

You have the option to join my reader's newsletter on the same page.

FINAL THOUGHTS & TIPS.

WE'VE COVERED A LOT OF GROUND.

This book was written in a positive, light, and conversational style in the hope of making a sometimes-difficult topic readable for readers from any background. If you've read to the finish line, you've covered a lot of ground, including:

- The basics of how Google works.
- Google's ranking factors in 2023 according to industry studies.
- Keyword research.
- Improving your site's load speed.
- Optimizing keywords into your pages.
- Essentials for supporting mobile users.
- Optimizing user behavior.
- Google's official quality guidelines updated in December 2022.
- Link building - examples of beginner and advanced strategies.
- Link building - how to get featured in the mainstream news for free.
- Social media and SEO.
- Web analytics basics.
- Fixing common SEO problems and solutions.
- Local SEO essentials.

- Targeting rich snippets.
- Steps to secure your website with HTTPS encryption.
- Google's Core Web Vitals.
- Major Google updates such as the February Product Reviews update and March 2023 Core Update.
- The vicious battle between ChatGPT and Google's Bard.
- Google Analytics Updates in 2023.
- The upcoming Cookieless Tracking Update in 2024.
- Staying ahead of future updates.
- Basics for Google Ads campaigns.
... and much more.

Congratulations on being a positive and proactive reader and finishing this book! The knowledge we've covered is more than enough to get started in SEO. It's also enough to increase rankings, traffic, and sales if you already have moderate levels of success.

Don't forget why we learn SEO in the first place, details are important, but don't get bogged down in them. I often see many readers, business owners, and marketers lost in endless articles, forums, and blog posts on SEO, and not making any progress with their projects.

If there is one thing I want you to take away from this book, it isn't an appetite for details. I want you to finish this book with a propensity to action. Of all the readers I encounter, the most successful are those with a positive and proactive attitude, who put their new knowledge into action.

Remember, what matters most is that you optimize your site well enough to beat competitors, make sales, and grow your business. If your site shows stronger signals to Google than competitors, you will win in the rankings. Most importantly, have fun with it, make it your own, and be positive and proactive!

~

CORRECTIONS & FEEDBACK.

I want this book to be the best for all readers, which is why I'm open to feedback from all readers and use feedback in updates as much as possible. If you are unhappy for any reason, noticed a mistake, or want something included, give me a chance to fix it, and email me at adam@simpleeffectiveness.com. I'll be happy to hear from you. Seriously!

WHAT TO DO NEXT.

Would you like more books in this simple and easy-to-understand format? Please take a quick moment and leave a review on Amazon, it will encourage me to get my next book out! I read all reader reviews and just a small moment of your time will sincerely make my day.

For Kindle readers, swipe to the next page and rate this book.

- Adam Clarke

Made in the USA
Coppell, TX
01 August 2023

19865817R00134